IMAGES
of England

GILLINGHAM FOOTBALL CLUB

Excelsior FC, *c.* 1890. The club met with such success in local league and cup competitions that it was decided that a professional club should be formed. Thus New Brompton FC came into being.

IMAGES
of England

Gillingham Football Club

Compiled by
Roger Triggs

First published 1999

Tempus Publishing Limited
The Mill, Brimscombe Port,
Stroud, Gloucestershire, GL5 2QG

ISBN 0 7524 1567 0

Typesetting and origination by
Tempus Publishing Limited
Printed in Great Britain by
Midway Clark Printing, Wiltshire

Some other football titles from Tempus Publishing:

Anfield Voices
Bristol Rovers FC
Bury FC
Cardiff City FC 1899-1947
Cardiff City FC 1947-1971
Celtic FC 1887-1967
Charlton Athletic FC
Crewe Alexandra FC
Crystal Palace FC
Exeter City FC
Heart of Midlothian FC
Newport County FC 1912-1960
Oxford United FC
Plymouth Argyle FC
Rangers FC
Reading FC
Roker Park Voices
Sheffield United FC
Stoke City FC
Sunderland FC
Swansea Town FC 1912-1964
Tranmere Rovers FC

Contents

About the Author

Although Roger Triggs was born in Hampstead, his family roots are Gillingham through and through. His great-grandfather originated from the town, as did his late father, and it was no surprise when his family moved to Rainham when he was aged only three.

Two years later, he saw his first 'Gills' match, the 5-4 home victory over Gateshead on the opening day of the 1959/60 season, although he spent most of the match running up and down the Gillingham End terracing! He became an avid collector of statistics and photographs whilst still at school, during which time he compiled his first history of the club.

In 1976, he starting writing articles for the matchday programme, an activity which spanned the next nineteen years. During this time, he published two books on the club: *Gillingham FC – A Chronology 1893-1984*, which was part of the Gillingham Local History Series issued by Kent County Libraries, and *Priestfield Profiles – A Who's Who of Gillingham's Football League Players 1950-88*. In 1993, together with Andy Bradley, he helped with the club's highly acclaimed centenary book *Home of the Shouting Men*.

Employed by Medway Council, he also finds time for the occasional game of cricket, and researching his family tree. At the present time he is working on a complete 'who's who' of Gillingham's Football League players for the periods 1920 to 1938 and 1950 to 1999. He is still looking for photographs of players from the earlier period – if anybody can help, please contact him at no. 115 Sunnymead Avenue, Gillingham, Kent ME7 2EA, or telephone him on Medway (01634) 851326.

Introduction

At the turn of the century, it was generally agreed that no club from Kent would rise to great footballing heights until a well-populated area could maintain a top class team. Several attempts had been made to found such a club around the Medway area. Rochester was the first, followed by The Royal Engineers,who were beaten FA Cup finalists in 1872 and 1874, before winning the competition in 1875 by defeating Old Etonians. Then Chatham burst upon the scene, with more glory in the FA Cup, before it was the turn of New Brompton's band of enthusiasts to challenge the best sides.

The club was the pioneer of professionalism in the South, and changed their status even before teams like Arsenal. Accepted into the Southern League Second Division in 1894, the club was promoted in its first season and they remained in the top flight until 1920. Although championships eluded the club during this period, on the whole it was a successful struggle against adversity, which was mainly due to poor finances. Good players had to be sold to balance the books, whilst new ones had to obtained for next to nothing.

In 1920, along with the other Southern League First Division clubs, Gillingham became one of the original founders of Division Three of the Football League. Some good seasons were followed by poor ones and, although the club were forced to seek re-election on five occasions, it still came as a surprise when, in 1938, they were voted out of the League in favour of Ipswich Town. They decided to continue on in other football circles and, during the period between 1944 and 1950, won nearly every honour available to them.

When the Southern Section of the Football League was enlarged in 1950, the club rightly regained their place among the country's elite. Eight years later, they became founder members of Division Four and gained their only championship in the 1963/64 season. Gillingham retained Division Three status for seven years but, after near escapes in 1968/69 and 1969/70, relegation finally happened in the next season.

Promotion was once again achieved in 1973/74 and the club remained in Division Three for the next fifteen years, although they did come close to gaining promotion in 1978/79 and 1986/87. After relegation in 1989, the following six years saw Gillingham find themselves in the all-too-familiar position of falling attendances, financial problems and boardroom changes until finally, in January 1995, the club was put into receivership.

Since Paul Scally took over during the summer of 1995, the club has taken on a new lease of life. Promotion was gained at the first attempt (with attendance figures up by over 100%) and in each subsequent season the club has grown in stature and profile. Four years ago, who would have imagined that we would sell a player for over £1 million and purchase two for a combined total of £1.1 million?

This is not a concise history of the club – that was covered in *Home of the Shouting Men* – but these photographs and other items will, I'm sure, bring back memories to everybody who has an interest in the 'Gills'.

Roger Triggs
February 1999

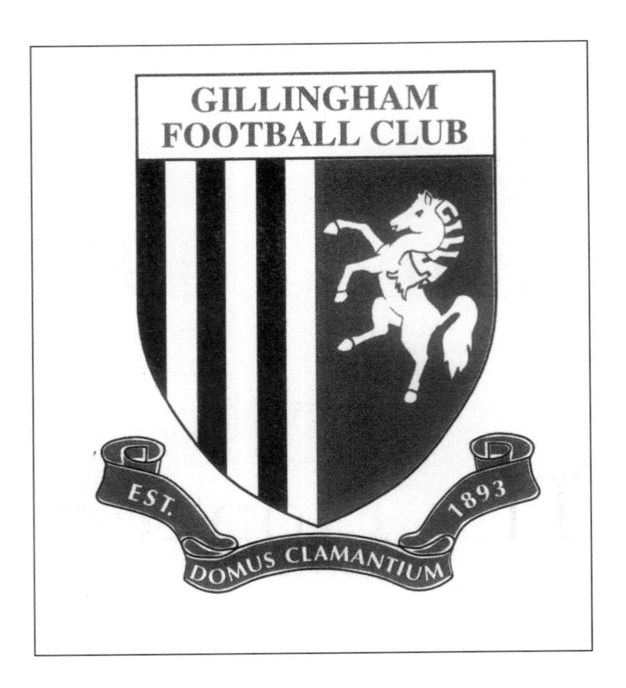

Acknowledgements

Although most of the contents of this book come from my own collection of photographs and memorabilia, I appreciate the help given to me by the following organisations and people: The Colorsport Photo Agency, Gillingham Borough Council (now incorporated within Medway Council), The *Kent Messenger* group of newspapers (Tony Hudd), The *Medway News & Standard* (Lance Morgan and Andy Bradley), Charlie Burtenshaw, Paul Howard, John Letley, Gloria Liptrott (Gillingham FC), Chris McLeod (Medway Council), Gwen Poynter (Gillingham FC), Richard Sellers, Keith Slater, John Swarby (Gillingham FC) and Pam Tyler.

One

The Pioneers

The Napier Arms in Britton Street, Gillingham. This was where, on Thursday 18 May 1893, New Brompton Football Club was formed. In 1993, exactly one hundred years after the original meeting, a plaque was unveiled in the public house to celebrate the club's centenary. The following two pages show the minutes taken from that first meeting.

At a public meeting held at the Napier Arms Inn New Brompton, this day, to consider the question of the formation of a Company to be called the New Brompton Football ~~Ground~~ Club Compy Limited.

It was proposed by Mr H. G. Croneen, seconded by Mr Crump That the High Constable of Gillingham (J. R. Featherby Esq:) take the Chair

The Minutes of the last meeting were passed as read

Mr H. G. Croneen as Chairman of a Committee nominated to view and report upon various sites offered to the Company having read his report It was proposed by Mr Partridge and seconded by Mr Reed that Mr Lipop's tender be read with the others

Proposed as an Amendment by Mr Parker and seconded by Mr W. Croneen that it be not entertained.

There voted for the amendment _22
For the original proposition — 30

Tenders having been read by Mr H. G. Croneen It was proposed by Mr Pacely seconded by Mr Richardson that the tender of Messrs Filley & Randall be accepted - Carried.

Proposed by Mr Thompson seconded by Mr P. Little that the following Gentlemen be elected

a Committee to promote the Company
Mr James Barnes of The Railway Hotel New Brompton Licenced Victualler.
Mr Frederick Bloor of High Street New Brompton Wardrobe dealer.
Mr William Herbert Checkefield of The Napier Arms Inn New Brompton Licenced Victualler
Mr Horace George Croneen of High Street New Brompton Jeweller
Mr Walter Croneen of The Viscount Harding Inn New Brompton
Mr Henry William Elliot of Napier Road New Brompton Builder
Mr Albert William Partridge of New Brompton Station Master
Mr Richard James Passby of Beacon Court Canterbury Road New Brompton Wine Merchant.
Mr George Randall of High Street New Brompton Pawnbroker
Mr Alfred Concannon Richardson of Windmill Road New Brompton Quarter Master Sergeant R.E.
Mr William Cornish Snow of Canterbury Street New Brompton Builder.
Edwin Charles Warren Esq: High Street New Brompton Medical Practitioner

Proposed by Mr H. G. Croneen Seconded by Mr Evans that the High Constable of Gillingham for the time being be President of the New Brompton Football Club.

Chairman.

The New Brompton side pictured with the Chatham Charity Cup, which they won during the 1893/94 season. From left to right, back row: Murray, Jenner, Taylor, Auld, Liddle. Middle row: Hibbard, Ashdown, Hutcheson (Captain), Buckland, James. Front row: Tyler, Rowlands.

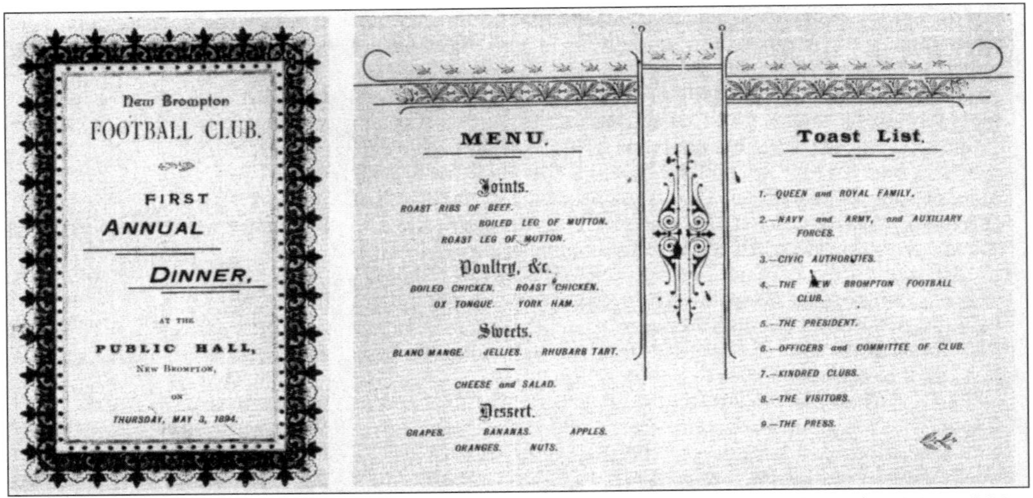

New Brompton
FOOTBALL CLUB.

FIRST
ANNUAL
DINNER,

AT THE
PUBLIC HALL,
NEW BROMPTON,
ON
THURSDAY, MAY 3, 1894.

MENU.

Joints.
ROAST RIBS OF BEEF.
BOILED LEG OF MUTTON.
ROAST LEG OF MUTTON.

Poultry, &c.
BOILED CHICKEN. ROAST CHICKEN.
OX TONGUE. YORK HAM.

Sweets.
BLANC MANGE. JELLIES. RHUBARB TART.

CHEESE and SALAD.

Dessert.
GRAPES. BANANAS. APPLES.
ORANGES. NUTS.

Toast List.

1.—QUEEN and ROYAL FAMILY.
2.—NAVY and ARMY, and AUXILIARY FORCES.
3.—CIVIC AUTHORITIES.
4.—THE NEW BROMPTON FOOTBALL CLUB.
5.—THE PRESIDENT.
6.—OFFICERS and COMMITTEE OF CLUB.
7.—KINDRED CLUBS.
8.—THE VISITORS.
9.—THE PRESS.

To celebrate their first season and professional status – which had been adopted in May 1894 – New Brompton FC held their first-ever dinner.

New Brompton before their first-ever game as a professional club. Having joined the Southern League, they were placed in the Second Division and started the season with a 6-0 victory at Sheppey United. From left to right, back row: Ashdown, Carr (Referee), Jenner, Pellatt, James, Meager, Auld, Murray (Trainer). Front row: Manning, Buckland, Hutcheson, Rule, Dickenson. Brompton went on to finish as champions and, after defeating Swindon Town in a test match, won promotion to the Southern League First Division.

One of the leading figures in the development of the club was James Barnes. The landlord of the Railway Hotel in New Brompton, he was one of the original directors and became chairman of the club from 1902 until 1912.

New Brompton, with the Chatham Charity Cup, 1895/96. Whilst in the Southern League First Division, the club finished mid-table. From left to right, back row: (Directors) Evans, Partridge, Barnes, Watson, Checksfield. Third row: Murray (Trainer), Watchurst (Treasurer), Manning, Hutcheson, Gascoigne, Meager, Clother (Secretary). Second row (seated): Warren (Chairman), Thomas, Buckland, Pellatt (Captain), McNamee, Bruce, Parker. Front row: Cochrane, Gladwell, Walker Cockrill.

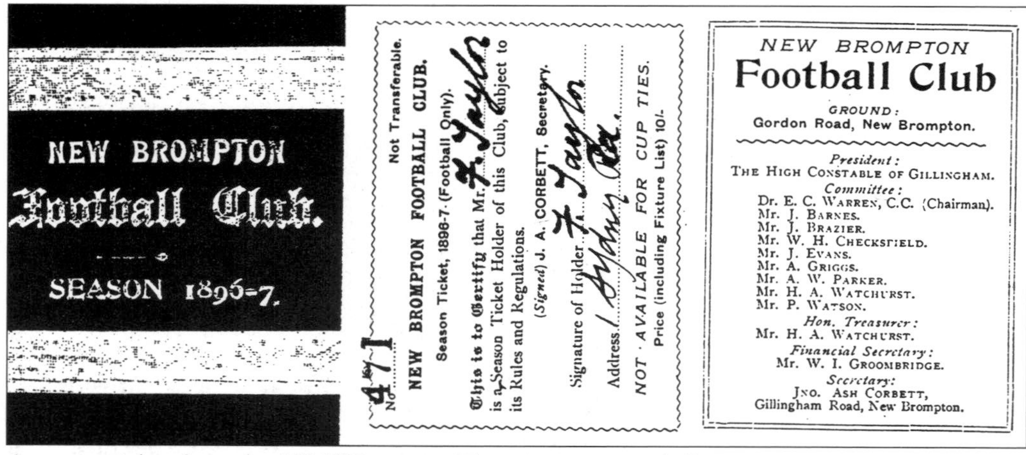

NEW BROMPTON
Football Club.
SEASON 1896-7.

No. 471
Not Transferable.
NEW BROMPTON FOOTBALL CLUB.
Season Ticket, 1896-7. (Football Only).
This is to Certify that Mr. F. Taylor
is a Season Ticket Holder of this Club, subject to its Rules and Regulations.
(Signed) J. A. CORBETT, Secretary.
Signature of Holder F. Taylor
Address 1 Sydney Rd.
NOT AVAILABLE FOR CUP TIES.
Price (including Fixture List) 10/-.

NEW BROMPTON
Football Club
GROUND:
Gordon Road, New Brompton.
President:
The High Constable of Gillingham.
Committee:
Dr. E. C. Warren, C.C. (Chairman).
Mr. J. Barnes.
Mr. J. Brazier.
Mr. W. H. Checksfield.
Mr. J. Evans.
Mr. A. Griggs.
Mr. A. W. Parker.
Mr. H. A. Watchurst.
Mr. P. Watson.
Hon. Treasurer:
Mr. H. A. Watchurst.
Financial Secretary:
Mr. W. I. Groombridge.
Secretary:
Jno. Ash Corbett,
Gillingham Road, New Brompton.

A season ticket from the 1896/97 season. The price was ten shillings.

New Brompton before the local derby at Chatham on Saturday 17 October 1896. In front of a crowd of 7,000, the game finished in a 3-3 draw. From left to right, back row: Gentle, Groombridge (Financial Secretary), Shaves, Corbett (Secretary), Pellatt, Watson, Gascoigne, Cockrill, Carroll, Bruce. Front row: Thomas, Frettingham, Hutcheson, Gladwell, Peters.

Ace marksman Jack Frettingham signed from Lincoln City in June 1896 and was leading scorer for five consecutive seasons from 1897 until 1902. Including FA Cup matches, he scored 76 goals in 180 appearances for the club. He tragically died in May 1904, as a result of an injury received whilst playing in the Derby area.

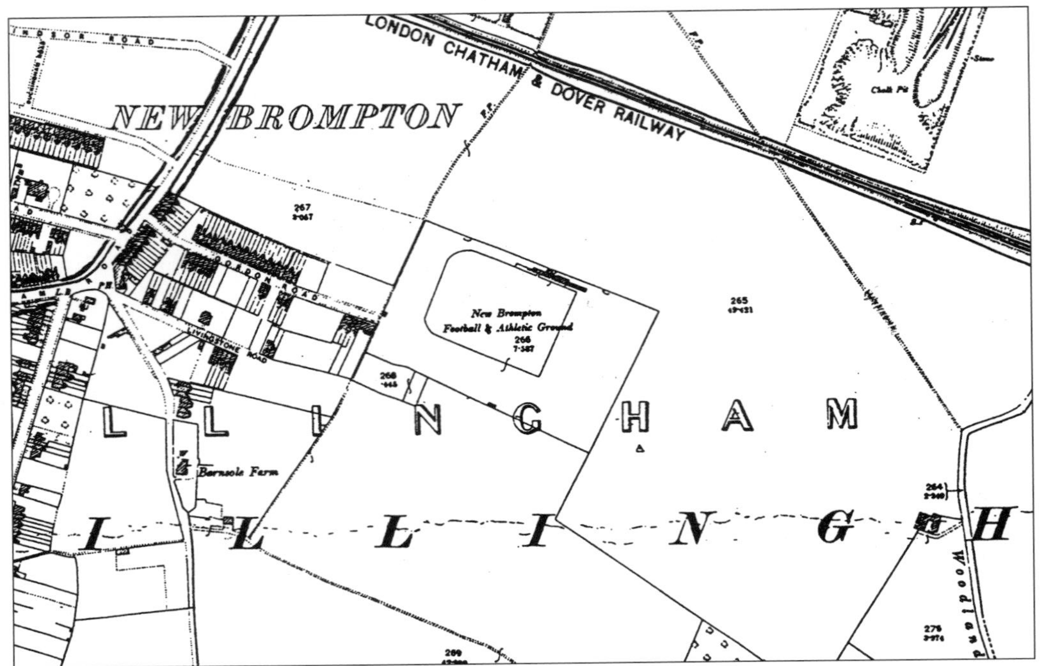

At the turn of the twentieth century, the area around New Brompton's ground was still sparsely built on: only parts of Gordon Road and Livingstone Road had been developed. With the formation of Gillingham Borough Council in 1903 and Brompton's incorporation into the new borough, the population increased by over fifty per cent, due to rows and rows of new dwellings in the vicinity of the ground.

Centre half Jim Atherton, who provided sterling service for the club between 1898 and 1904, having been signed from Kettering. He made 139 appearances, but is probably best remembered for his winning goal against Woolwich Arsenal (now Arsenal) in the FA Cup during the 1899/1900 season. This third (qualifying) round tie lasted five matches and was eventually settled at Gravesend by Atherton's strike, which was the only goal of the game. He died in December 1915 and was buried in the new cemetery in Gillingham, now situated in Woodlands Road.

No. of Certificate 425 Transfer No. of Shares 10

New Brompton Football Club Company

LIMITED.

INCORPORATED UNDER "THE COMPANIES ACTS, 1862 to 1890."

CAPITAL £1500 IN 1500 SHARES OF £1 EACH.

This is to Certify that Thomas Hill Esq

of 93 Copenhagen Road New Brompton Kent

is the Registered Proprietor of Ten fully paid-up Shares of £1 each, Numbered 129 to 138 in the above-named Company, subject to the Memorandum and Articles of Association of the said Company.

Given under the Common Seal of the said Company the 14th day of April, 1900

W. H. Checksfield
W. J. Waters, } Directors.

W. A. Groombridge Secretary.

Printed by Charles Doubble, 14, Serjeants' Inn, Temple, London, E.C

A copy of a share certificate for ten shares, issued in April 1900. They were acquired by Mr Thomas Hill and gave him the right to serve as a director of the club, a position he held from 1901 until 1907.

Alf Milward was one of the leading players in the New Brompton side around 1900. Signed in July 1901 from Southampton, he had made his name at Everton, with whom he won the League Championship in 1891 and the FA Cup twice, in 1893 and 1897. He also won 4 caps for England.

New Brompton FC, 1902/03. The team had a highly satisfactory season in the Southern League, finishing in sixth position, as well as reaching the sixth qualifying round of the FA Cup. From left to right, back row: Killean, Daw, Archer. Middle row: Watchurst (Treasurer), McCurdy, Raisbeck, Goldie, Elliott, Lofthouse (Trainer), Groombridge (Secretary). Front row: Bradbury, Smith, Milward, Satterthwaite, Dunkley. On ground: Leigh.

Former England junior international Joe Elliott joined New Brompton during the summer of 1902 from Preston North End. A virtual ever-present during his four years with the club (146 appearances), he later became licensee of The Cricketers public house in Sturdee Avenue.

New Brompton, 1903/04. It was a poor season in terms of results and goalscoring. The team only won six games, scoring 26 goals from 34 Southern League fixtures. They finished third from bottom. From left to right, back row: (Directors) Hill, Evans, Barker, Winter, Barnes (Chairman), Featherby (Mayor), (Directors) Pearce, Checksfield, Godden, Swain (Treasurer). Middle row: Groombridge (Secretary), McCurdy, Raisbeck, Goldie, Clutterbuck, Elliott, White. Front row: Craddock (Trainer), Robertson, Stevenson, Boucher, Smith, Singleton, Unthank (Assistant Trainer).

William Ironside Groombridge. One of the club's most loyal and dedicated officials in the early years, he joined New Brompton as financial secretary in April 1896. A year later, he became secretary and held that position until June 1923, when he handed in his resignation. Two years earlier, he had been rewarded for twenty-five years' service with a testimonial match against Arsenal.

New Brompton, 1904/05. They finished in a mid-table position, having at one stage reached the dizzy heights of third place. From left to right, back row: Groombridge (Secretary), Craddock (Trainer), Watts, Barnes (Chairman), Griffiths, Swain (Treasurer). Middle row: Elliott, McKie, Boucher, Turner, Lagar, White. Front row: Barnfather, Leigh, Morris.

Star full-back Joseph Walton. Signed from non-League football in the North East, he developed into an enterprising and no-nonsense player, who soon attracted the big clubs to the Gordon Road enclosure. He eventually moved to Chelsea during the summer of 1906, for a fee of £200 – big money in those days!

Players and officials of the club, 1905/06. It turned out to be New Brompton's worst season since gaining promotion to the Southern League First Division in 1895. Finding the net was the problem, with only 20 goals being scored, and the club finished next to bottom in the table.

New Brompton FC, before the 1906/07 season. This was much better than the previous term, mainly due to the goalscoring form of Danny Cunliffe (15) and Jim Hartley (10). From left to right, back row: Checksfield (Director), Crumbie (Director), Paton (Doctor), Craddock (Trainer), Hill (Director). Standing: Evans (Director), Edwards (Mayor), Walker, Martin, Floyd, Barnes (Chairman), Pearce (Director). Seated: Groombridge (Secretary), Lloyd, Maven, Elliott, Morgan, Swain (Treasurer). On ground: Warrington, Cunliffe, Lee, Marriott, Hartley, Smith.

Speedy winger Steve Smith, who was an ever-present during the 1906/07 season following his transfer from Portsmouth. Originally with Aston Villa, he had helped them win the League Championship in 1893/94, 1895/96, 1896/97, 1898/99 and 1899/1900 as well as the FA Cup in 1895. A superb passer of the ball, he was New Brompton's player/manager from December 1906 until the summer of 1908, when he retired from the game.

New Brompton's squad for the 1908/09 season. From left to right, back row: Crumbie (Director), Negus (Director), W. Henderson, Bateup, Hales, Craddock (Trainer). Middle row: Simmons (Mayor), Arthurs, Maven, W.P. Henderson, Fullarton, Barnes (Chairman). Front row: Groombridge (Secretary), Reynolds, Wood, Whyman, Powell, Reid, Pickett, Swain (Treasurer). A final placing of seventh in the Southern League table represented a much better performance over the season, which also resulted in the average home gate being over 5,000.

Centre half Fred Maven, who joined New Brompton from Newcastle United (his home town club) in September 1905 and went on to make a total of 118 first team appearances. He moved to Fulham during the summer of 1909, where he gained a reputation as a goalscoring defender. He returned to Priestfield in the 1930s when he became manager.

New Brompton FC, 1909/10. Thanks to the goalscoring exploits of dockyard worker Albert Court (22) and ex-Hull striker John Taylor (19), the club scored a total of 76 goals in this Southern League campaign, to finish in a respectable mid-table position. From left to right, back row: Nobbs, Sutherland, Bateup, McArthur, Court. Middle row: Crumbie (Director), Mahon, Johnson, Strang, Higgins, Fullarton, Crawley (Director). Front row: Ryenolds, Satterthwaite, Taylor, Vinall (Mayor), Reid, Beale, Pickett.

Out go the familiar black and white stripes and in comes the dazzling red and blue shirts, with the borough's coat of arms as the new club badge. Although the name of the club was not officially changed to Gillingham until a meeting on 17 July 1913, this was the first season the club played under their new name.

Gillingham FC, 1913/14. Ex-Liverpool striker Sam Gilligan had been appointed player/manager and, under his control, the club finished in a comfortable mid-table position. More importantly though, attendances rose to an average of 6,500. From left to right, back row: MacDonald Judge (Surgeon), Crumbie (Director), Checksfield (Director), Mosley, Bailey, Leslie, Wright (Trainer), Wood (Director), Evans (Vice-chairman). Middle row: Crawley (Chairman), Pearce (Supporters Association), Hughes (Supporters Association), Mahon, Lee, Johnson, Johns, Parker (Director), Levy (Director), Groombridge (Secretary). Front row: Pinkney, Gilligan, Swain (Mayor), Glen, Hafekost, Caldwell.

Local businessman Edward Crawley, who served as a director of the club from 1907 to 1939. He was also chairman of the club from 1912 until 1922.

Due to the increased attendance figures, the directors decided it was time for a new grandstand to be built. *Above*: An artist's impression of the new building, which was completed in November 1914. *Below*: Unfortunately, just over a month later, it was reduced to rubble after strong winds on the night of 29 December. It was not until the following March that the damage was repaired.

Gillingham's last season in the Southern League ended in disaster as the club finished bottom of the table – during which time they used a total of thirty-nine players to try and find a winning formula! From left to right, back row: Cartwright, Branfield, Leslie, Chalmers. Middle row: R. Steel, A. Lee, B. Read, Kennedy, A. Steel, Levy (Director), Groombridge (Secretary). Front row: Crawley (Chairman), (Referee), Wood, H. Lee, Mahon, Redpath, Kelly, Wood (Director).

Goalkeeper Jack Branfield. Born in Gillingham in October 1891, Jack excelled in schoolboy and local football, before joining the club in November 1919. He served the club for their first two seasons in the Football League, before moving to Sheppey United in June 1922.

Despite their poor form during the 1919/20 season, Gillingham at least held Portsmouth, the eventual champions, to a goal-less draw at home on Saturday 13 March. This illustration is one of many that were used in the local newspaper during the course of the season.

Two

Election to the Football League

A crowd of 11,500 packed Priestfield to see Gillingham's first Football League fixture against Southampton on Saturday 28 August 1920. This is the historic line-up from that fixture. From left to right (players only), back row: Robertson, Battiste, Baxter, Wigmore, Sisson. Front row: Holt, Hall, Branfield, Gilbey, Roe, Gore. Tom Gilbey netted Gillingham's goal in a 1-1 draw, but it was to be a bad season and Gillingham finished in bottom position.

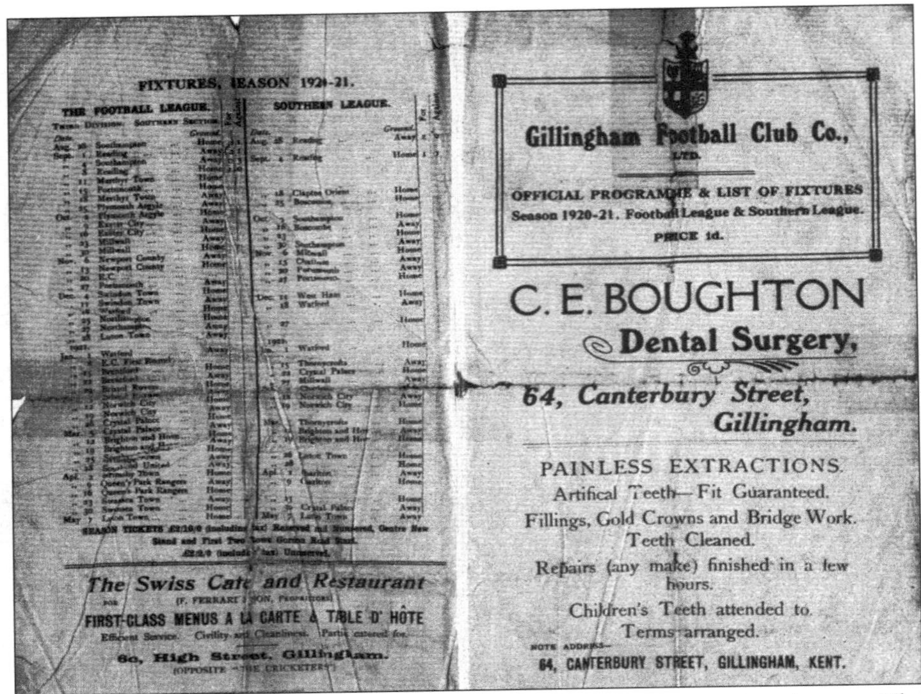

FIXTURES, SEASON 1920-21.

THE FOOTBALL LEAGUE. Third Division. Southern Section.

SOUTHERN LEAGUE.

SEASON TICKETS £2/10/0 (including tax) Reserved and Numbered, Centre New Stand and First Two Rows Gordon Road Stand. £2/2/0 (including tax) Unreserved.

The Swiss Cafe and Restaurant

(F. FERRARI & SON, Proprietors)

FIRST-CLASS MENUS A LA CARTE & TABLE D' HÔTE

Efficient Service. Civility and Cleanliness. Parties catered for.

60, High Street, Gillingham.

(OPPOSITE "THE CRICKETERS")

Gillingham Football Club Co., LTD.

OFFICIAL PROGRAMME & LIST OF FIXTURES

Season 1920-21. Football League & Southern League.

PRICE 1d.

C. E. BOUGHTON

Dental Surgery,

64, Canterbury Street, Gillingham.

PAINLESS EXTRACTIONS.

Artifical Teeth—Fit Guaranteed.

Fillings, Gold Crowns and Bridge Work.

Teeth Cleaned.

Repairs (any make) finished in a few hours.

Children's Teeth attended to.

Terms arranged.

NOTE ADDRESS—

64, CANTERBURY STREET, GILLINGHAM, KENT.

One of the earliest Gillingham Football League home programmes in existence. The four page issue (priced at one old penny) was for the game against Merthyr Town on Saturday 11 September 1920. A crowd of nearly 10,000 saw the match, which finished goal-less.

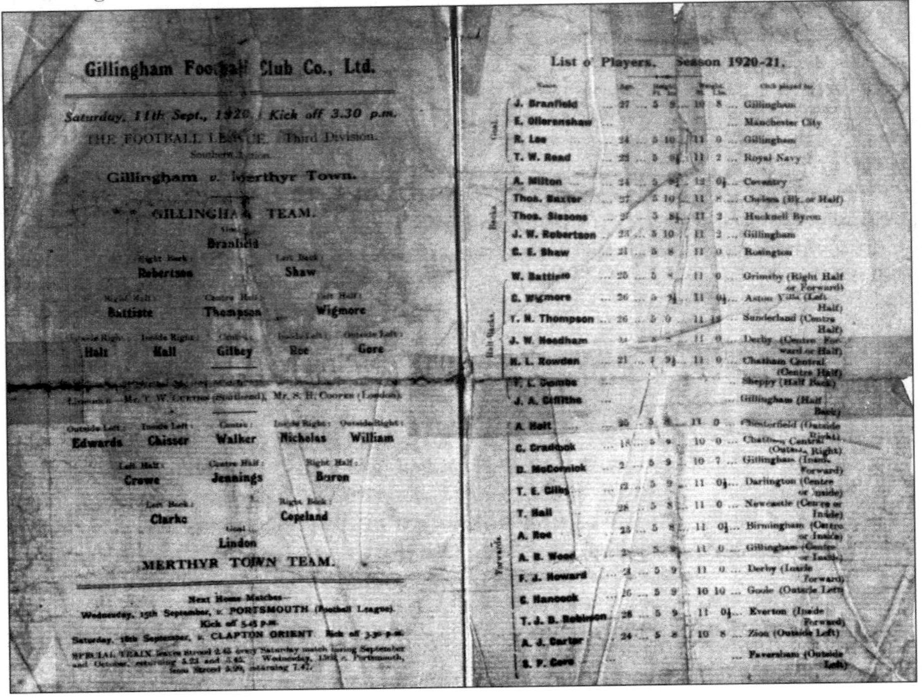

Gillingham Football Club Co., Ltd.

Saturday, 11th Sept., 1920. Kick off 3.30 p.m.

THE FOOTBALL LEAGUE. Third Division. Southern Section.

Gillingham v. Merthyr Town.

GILLINGHAM TEAM.

Goal: Branfield

Right Back: Robertson — Left Back: Shaw

Right Half: Battiste — Centre Half: Thompson — Left Half: Wigmore

Outside Right: Holt — Inside Right: Hall — Centre: Gilbey — Inside Left: Roe — Outside Left: Gore

Linesmen—Mr. T. W. Curtis (Southend), Mr. S. H. Cooper (London).

Outside Left: Edwards — Inside Left: Chisser — Centre: Walker — Inside Right: Nicholas — Outside Right: William

Left Half: Crowe — Centre Half: Jennings — Right Half: Baron

Left Back: Clarke — Right Back: Copeland

Goal: Lindon

MERTHYR TOWN TEAM.

Next Home Matches—

Wednesday, 15th September, v. PORTSMOUTH (Football League). Kick off 5.45 p.m.

Saturday, 18th September, v. CLAPTON ORIENT. Kick off 3.30 p.m.

List o' Players. Season 1920-21.

	Name	Age	Height ft. in.	Weight st. lbs.	Club played for
Goal	J. Branfield	27	5 9	10 8	Gillingham
	E. Ollerenshaw				Manchester City
	R. Lee	24	5 10	11 0	Gillingham
	T. W. Read	22	5 9½	11 2	Royal Navy
Backs	A. Milton	24	5 9½	12 0½	Coventry
	Thos. Baxter	27	5 10	11 8	Chelsea (Bk. or Half)
	Thos. Sissons	[illegible]	5 8½	11 2	Hucknell Byron
	J. W. Robertson	23	5 10	11 2	Gillingham
	C. E. Shaw	21	5 8	11 0	Rosington
Half-Backs	W. Battiste	25	5 8	11 0	Grimsby (Right Half or Forward)
	C. Wigmore	26	5 9½	11 0½	Aston Villa (Left Half)
	T. H. Thompson	26	5 0	11 12	Sunderland (Centre Half)
	J. W. Needham	[illegible]	[illegible]	11 0	Derby (Centre Forward or Half)
	H. L. Rowden	21	5 9½	11 0	Chatham Central (Centre Half)
	F. L. Dombe				Sheppy (Half Back)
	J. A. Griffiths				Gillingham (Half Back)
Forwards	A. Holt	25	5 8	11 0	Chesterfield (Outside Right)
	C. Craddock	18	5 9	10 0	Chatham Central (Outside Right)
	D. McCormick	2[illegible]	5 9	10 7	Gillingham (Inside Forward)
	T. E. Gilbey	[illegible]	5 9	11 0½	Darlington (Centre or Inside)
	T. Hall	28	5 8	11 0	Newcastle (Centre or Inside)
	A. Roe	23	5 8	11 0½	Birmingham (Centre or Inside)
	A. B. Wood	2[illegible]	5 8	11 0	Gillingham (Centre or Inside)
	F. J. Howard	21	5 9	11 0	Derby (Inside Forward)
	C. Hancock	26	5 9	10 10	Goole (Outside Left)
	T. J. B. Robinson	28	5 9	11 0½	Everton (Inside Forward)
	A. J. Carter	24	5 8	10 8	Zion (Outside Left)
	S. P. Gore				Faversham (Outside Left)

More goals scored and less conceded meant that Gillingham had a much better time of it in the 1921/22 season. This is the team before the 2-0 home victory over Southampton on Saturday 3 September 1921. From left to right, back row: Simms, Marshall, Branfield, Waugh, Sisson, McAlphine. Front row: McMillan (Manager), Battiste, Freeman, Wood, Hall, Waterall, Kennedy (Trainer).

Left: Upon their entry into the Football League, former Derby County, Leicester Fosse and Bradford City player John McMillan was appointed manager. He spent badly in trying to keep the club afloat and was eventually sacked in August 1922. He passed away in November 1941. *Right*: Goalscoring inside forward Tommy Hall cost a club record fee of £1,000 when he came from Newcastle United in August 1920. In six seasons with the club, he scored 55 goals in 207 first team appearances, before becoming trainer in August 1926. He eventually returned to his native North East, where he became a licensee.

Gillingham FC line-up from 1922/23. Once again the club finished in the lower regions of the Division Three (South) table and only winning their final four games enabled the club to avoid re-election.

Left: Inside forward Charlie Freeman, who in 1922/23 finished as top League scorer for the second consecutive season. Signed from Chelsea during the summer of 1921, he moved on to Maidstone United in June 1923. He returned to Stamford Bridge in later life, where he was employed as groundsman until his retirement in 1953. *Right*: Scottish centre half John 'Jock' Henderson, who created a new club record during the 1922/23 season. He finished the campaign with nine League goals – of which all but one came from the penalty spot! Signed from Welsh club Mid-Rhonda during the summer of 1922, he stayed at Priestfield for two seasons before returning north of the border to join Dunfermline Athletic in July 1924.

Gillingham before their home game with Northampton Town on Saturday 6 October 1923. The match finished 1-1, with Tommy Hall netting in the first half. From left to right (players only), behind: Read, Robertson, Thompson, Hendrie, Needham, North. Front: Battiste, Cosgrove, Fox, Hall, Sinning.

Left: Goalkeeper Freddie Fox became the first and (to date) only Gillingham player to be selected for a full England international in May 1925. Secured from Swindon Town during the summer of 1922, his form between the posts soon bought plaudits from many quarters. In April 1925 he was transferred to Millwall for a fee of almost £500. *Right*: Former referee Harry Curtis was appointed secretary/manager of Gillingham in May 1923. A popular figure amongst players and supporters alike, success did not come and, after the club refused him a pay rise, he moved to Brentford in May 1926. In twenty-three years with the West London club he transformed them into a team that was challenging for the Division One title. He died in Warminster (Wiltshire) in January 1966.

Above left: Local-born full-back James 'Jock' Robertson, whose record of 358 League appearances stood for over thirty years. Demobbed by the army, he joined Gillingham in November 1919 and soon won a place in the side. He made his final appearance at Watford in October 1932, but went on to captain the reserves, as well as coaching the club's youngsters. He died at Rochester in December 1970. *Above right*: Centre forward Joe North equalled a club record of five goals in an FA Cup tie at Nunhead during the 1923/24 season. He was also good at the summer sport, appearing for Middlesex CCC in the County Championship. *Left*: Another local-born player who made good was speedy right-winger Dick Edmed. Signed from local football, he had made just a handful of appearances before Liverpool signed him in January 1926, for a club record fee of £1,800. After a long spell at Anfield and a short period with Bolton Wanderers, he returned to Priestfield after the Second World War to help train the club's reserve team. He died at Chatham in February 1983.

An Agreement made the 5th

day of May 1924 between Henry

Charles Curtis of 37 Linden Rd

Gillingham in the COUNTY OF Kent

the Secretary of and acting pursuant to Resolution and Authority for and on behalf of the Gillingham FOOTBALL CLUB,

of Kent (hereinafter referred to as the Club)

of the one part and Richard Alfred Edmed.

of 2. Featherby's Cottages Grange Rd Gillingham

in the County of Kent Professional Football Player

(hereinafter referred to as the Player) of the other part **Whereby** it is agreed as follows:—

1. The Player hereby agrees to play in an efficient manner and to the best of his ability for the Club.

2. The Player shall attend the Club's ground or any other place decided upon by the Club for the purposes of or in connection with his training as a Player pursuant to the instructions of the Secretary, Manager or Trainer of the Club or of such other person or persons as the Club may appoint.

3. The Player shall do everything necessary to get and keep himself in the best possible condition so as to render the most efficient service to the Club and will carry out all the training and other instructions of the Club through its representative officials.

4. The Player shall observe and be subject to all the Rules, Regulations and Bye-laws of The Football Association, and any other Association, League or Combination of which the Club shall be a member. And this Agreement shall be subject to any action which shall be taken by The Football Association under their Rules for the suspension or termination of the Football Season and if any such suspension or termination shall be decided upon the payment of wages shall likewise be suspended or terminated as the case may be.

5. The Player shall not engage in any business or live in any place which the Directors (or Committee) of the Club may deem unsuitable.

Dick Edmed's first professional contract with Gillingham, signed in May 1924.

Gillingham FC, 1924/25. From left to right, back row: Jones, Curtis (Manager), Robertson, Fox, Hendrie, Kane (Trainer), Hook, Vango. Front row: Chance, Ramsell, Brown, Hall, Berry, Marshall.

Left: Joint top-scorer during 1924/25 was inside forward Freddie Brown. Signed from Brighton & Hove Albion during the summer of 1924, he stayed for three seasons during which time he scored 32 goals in 108 first team appearances. He then returned to the North to play for his home-town club Gainsborough Trinity. *Right*: Outside right George Chance missed just two League games during the 1924/25 season, following his signing from Bristol Rovers. He moved to Millwall in April 1925, in a joint deal with goalkeeper Freddie Fox.

Gillingham FC, 1925/26. For the first time since being elected to the Football League, the club finished in the top half of the table. From left to right, back row: Brown, Robertson, Ferguson, Butler. Front row: Edmed, Marshall, McKee, Rutherford, Knight (Chairman), Hall, Berry, Reddock.

Left: Former Bristol Rovers and York player John Rutherford, a rugged central defender, made 84 League appearances for Gillingham in his three years with the club. He died tragically, at the early age of twenty-seven, in September 1930. *Right*: Wing-half Jim Nichol joined Gillingham from the Scottish club Glasgow Perthshire during the summer of 1925. His stylish displays soon bought the scouts flocking to Priestfield and eventually he joined Division One Portsmouth for a fee of £1,200 in November 1927.

Gillingham FC, 1927/28. This team did not have any problems scoring goals (62), but unfortunately conceded far too many (81). From left to right, back row: Rogers, Hall (Trainer), Robertson, Wood (Director), Hebden, Pickering, Hodnett, Hoskins (Manager). Front row: Meston, Hillier, Wilcox, Nichol, Arblaster, Bromage.

Left: Centre forward Jonah Wilcox, who was the club's only ever-present during the 1927/28 season, finished as top-scorer with 25 goals. *Right*: Goalkeeper George Hebden, who was a regular during the 1927/28 and 1928/29 seasons.

An unusual Gillingham line-up for this 1929/30 team picture! Fred Cheesmur, who scored a record six goals in one game against Merthyr Town in April 1930, is pictured third from left in the front row.

Left: Locally-born goalkeeper John Beby. After leaving Gillingham, he went on to play for Leicester City, Bristol Rovers and Crystal Palace. He later returned to play for Shorts Sports, as well as running The Cricketers public house in Layfield Avenue. He died in Rochester in April 1976. *Right*: John James Knight served as a director of the club between 1920 and 1947. He was chairman from 1922 until 1930. Four times elected mayor of Gillingham, Knight was made a Freeman of the Borough in 1926. He died in February 1948.

Gillingham FC, 1930/31. Manager Dick Hendrie is pictured second from the left in the back row.

Left: Former postman Fred Lester burst onto the scene during the 1930/31 season, making his debut whilst still an amateur. He remained with the club until October 1937, when, after 201 League appearances, he joined Sheffield Wednesday. *Right*: Goalscoring winger Billy Death was signed from Exeter City in August 1930.

Gillingham FC, 1932/33. This side finished seventh in the Division Three (South) table – the club's highest position since election to the League in 1920. From left to right, back row: Ure (Trainer), Forbes, Maven (Manager), Jackson, Bethell, Holland, Collins, Kidd, Lester, Gellatly, Crumbie (Chairman). Front row: Armfield, Purcell, Nicol, Raleigh, Liddle.

Left: Centre forward George Nicol equalled the club's goalscoring record during the 1932/33 season, with 25 goals. A former butcher by trade, he had previously appeared for Manchester United and Brighton & Hove Albion. *Right*: Full-back Richard Jackson was signed from Rotherham in August 1932 and was a regular in the side for two seasons. He later owned a greengrocers shop just off Gillingham High Street.

Just one defeat in the last ten games enabled Gillingham to avoid having to apply for re-election at the end of the 1934/35 season. From left to right, back row: Ure (Trainer), Randle, Robinson, Marsden, Harvey, Wiggins, Kidd, Maven (Manager). Front row: Bethell, Anstiss, Syred, Baldwin, Varty.

Inside forward Sim Raleigh (left) tragically lost his life as a result of an injury sustained in the home game against Brighton & Hove Albion on 1 December 1934. Midway through the first half, he clashed heads with Albion's centre half Paul Mooney (right). He collapsed just after half-time and, although surgeons tried to save his life, he died in St Barts Hospital at 9.50 pm that day.

Sim Raleigh's funeral was held in Hull, his home town. *Above*: The arrival of the funeral procession at the church. *Below*: His grave, which to this day is still lovingly looked after by his family.

Above Left: Centre forward Bill Baldwin finished as top scorer during the 1934/35 season, with 14 goals. In later life he gained fame as the 1965 All England Bowls Champion.

Above Right: Baldwin's strike partner was Harry Anstiss, who joined the club from Crewe Alexandra. He left Priestfield after just one season and went on to play for Tunbridge Wells Rangers and Cray Wanderers.

Left: Full-back Harry Marsden was another player who spent the 1934/35 season with the club, following his transfer from Brighton & Hove Albion.

Above: Goalkeeper Dave Whitelaw joined Gillingham during the summer of 1935 from Southend United and stayed with the club up to the outbreak of the Second World War.

Right: Skilful winger George Tadman who, although a locally-born man, was signed from Bristol Rovers in the summer of 1935. Top scorer that season with 19 goals, he was sold to Charlton Athletic in July 1936 for a fee of £1,000.

Gillingham's Kent League side of 1936/37. From left to right, back row: Harris, Hartley, Shardlow, Hopkins, Foreman, W. Wilson. Front row: Fowler, T. Wilson, Clancy, Wheeler, Dodds.

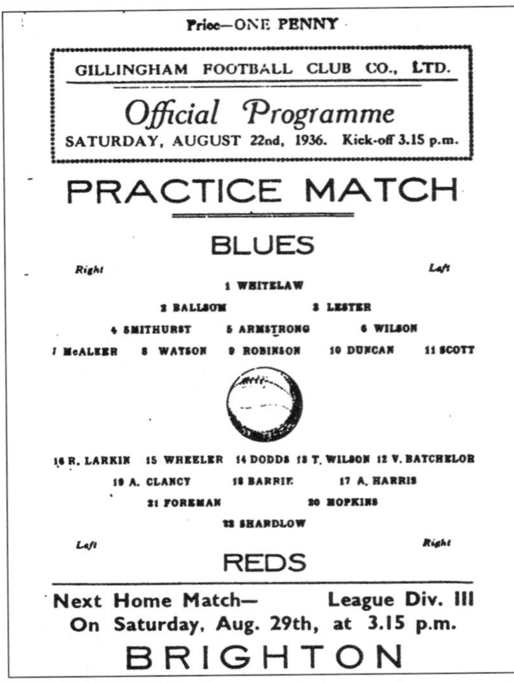

Price—ONE PENNY

GILLINGHAM FOOTBALL CLUB CO., LTD.

Official Programme

SATURDAY, AUGUST 22nd, 1936. Kick-off 3.15 p.m.

PRACTICE MATCH

BLUES

Right *Left*

1 WHITELAW

2 BALLSOM 3 LESTER

4 SMITHURST 5 ARMSTRONG 6 WILSON

7 McALEER 8 WATSON 9 ROBINSON 10 DUNCAN 11 SCOTT

16 R. LARKIN 15 WHEELER 14 DODDS 13 T. WILSON 12 V. BATCHELOR

19 A. CLANCY 18 BARRIE 17 A. HARRIS

21 FOREMAN 20 HOPKINS

22 SHARDLOW

Left *Right*

REDS

Next Home Match— League Div. III
On Saturday, Aug. 29th, at 3.15 p.m.

BRIGHTON

Left: No pre-season friendlies in those days! Most clubs had trials between probables and possibles, or, as this programme shows, Blues *v*. Reds. *Right*: Centre half Bill Armstrong was signed from Swindon Town during the summer of 1936. His solid displays at the heart of the defence soon made him a firm favourite and led to him being made captain.

First team players Tom Hopkins, Dave Whitelaw, Jim Dodds and Syd Hartley enjoy a break during pre-season training for the 1936/37 season.

Former Chelsea, Bristol Rovers and Lincoln City centre forward Albert Taylor joined Gillingham during the summer of 1937.

The 1937/38 season turned out to be a disaster for Gillingham. Under new manager Allan Ure, the club finished last in Division Three (South) and were forced to seek re-election for the fifth time. On this occasion they were not successful. However, in an emergency board meeting, the directors decided that the club should continue in non-League football. From left to right, back row: Ure (Manager), O'Neill, Hartley, Whitelaw, Tweed, Holland, Oxberry (Trainer). Front row: Watson, Wilson, Herbert, Neal, Fishlock, Ballsom.

The late Tom 'Tug' Wilson, one of the finest players ever to wear the blue shirt of Gillingham. Employed at Chatham dockyard, he turned down numerous offers of turning professional. A canny inside forward with a brilliant footballing brain, he joined Gillingham before the Second World War and remained with them until moving to Gravesend & Northfleet in October 1949.

Three

Into the Wilderness

After losing their Football League status in 1938, Gillingham were elected to the Southern League, where they finished in third place at the end of the 1938/39 season. Crowds were disappointing, despite the fact that the team only dropped three points at home throughout the campaign. This is part of the crowd for the home game against Bath City on Saturday 8 April 1939.

GILLINGHAM F.C. WILL CARRY ON

TO JOIN SOUTHERN LEAGUE

IMPORTANT DIRECTORS' MEETING TO-NIGHT

ALL MEDWAY TOWNS CLUB SUGGESTED

A BOMBSHELL has been dropped in Kent football circles and more particularly in the Medway Towns by the decision of the Football League at their meeting in London yesterday not to re-elect Gillingham to the Southern Section of the Third Division. Ipswich Town were elected in their place.

The voting was as follows: Ipswich Town 36 votes; Walsall 34; Gillingham 28.

The decision is in direct contrast to the recommendation of the Third Division Clubs made at their meeting three weeks ago. Gillingham were then recommended for re-election, being returned at the top of the poll with 18 votes against the eleven recorded each for Ipswich and Walsall.

Yesterday's meeting, however, was undoubtedly largely influenced by the fact, as Mr. C. E. Sutcliffe emphasised, that whereas Walsall have only once in their history had to apply for re-election, Gillingham have had to apply half-a-dozen times.

The news of the knock-out blow was received with consternation in the Medway Towns. The League decision has created a volume of protest and indignation and on all sides the view is expressed that the Kent club has not had a fair deal in view of the recommendation of their fellow Leaguers.

The directors of the Gillingham Club themselves are placed in a grave dilemma. Not only are they responsible for heavy debts, the legacy of past lean seasons, but in confident anticipation that the recommendation of the Third Division clubs would be acted upon they have incurred commitments for next season, especially in regard to signing new players, estimated to run into four figures.

There is, however, no appeal against the League decision and directors have now to consider what shall be done in the future.

Will the club go into voluntary liquidation or enter a minor league such as the Southern League or will a new club to embrace all the Medway Towns be floated?

The local press cutting that indicated the director's decision to carry on and compete in the Southern League for the 1938/39 season.

KENT COUNTY FOOTBALL ASSOCIATION

FOOTBALL

KENT SENIOR CUP–SEMI-FINAL

CHATHAM FOOTBALL GROUND
MAIDSTONE ROAD

SATURDAY, 18 MARCH, 1939
Kick-off 3.15 p.m.

NORTHFLEET UNITED
Right (Red Shirts) *Left*

E. Ditchburn
L. Codd Adams
McLean L. Coxford G. Piper
G. Sperrin L. Bennett A. E. Duffield Weston Revell

Referee: C. J. Biddle, Abbey Wood O *Linesmen:* W. J. Jones, Rochester
E. J. Holt, Gravesend

Scott Johnson Rowley Wilson McGee
Neal Armstrong Smith (J.)
Costello Bradbury
Whitelaw

GILLINGHAM
Left (Blue, White Collars and Cuffs) *Right*

In the event of a draw at the end of 90 minutes play extra time will NOT be played

H. S. Godfrey, Printer, High Street, Rainham, Kent

Above Left: The programme for the Kent Senior Cup semi-final against Northfleet at Chatham. Goals from Harry Rowley and 'Tug' Wilson saw Gillingham win 2-0 and go on to meet Tunbridge Wells Rangers in the final at Maidstone.

Above Right: In August 1939, former Everton centre half Archie Clark was appointed manager. However, after only a few weeks in office, war was declared and he and a number of the players went to work in the dockyard. It was to be nearly four years before football would return to Priestfield.

Right: Full-back Charlie Marks, who began a long association with the club in 1943. He played through the Kent, Southern and Football League until 1958. Renowned for having a powerful shot, his penalty kick in the home match against Northampton Town in February 1955 went straight through the netting!

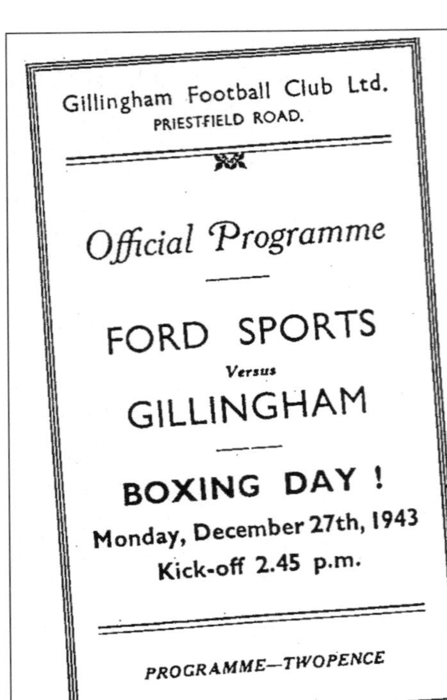

Gillingham Football Club Ltd.
PRIESTFIELD ROAD.

Official Programme

FORD SPORTS
Versus
GILLINGHAM

BOXING DAY !
Monday, December 27th, 1943
Kick-off 2.45 p.m.

PROGRAMME—TWOPENCE

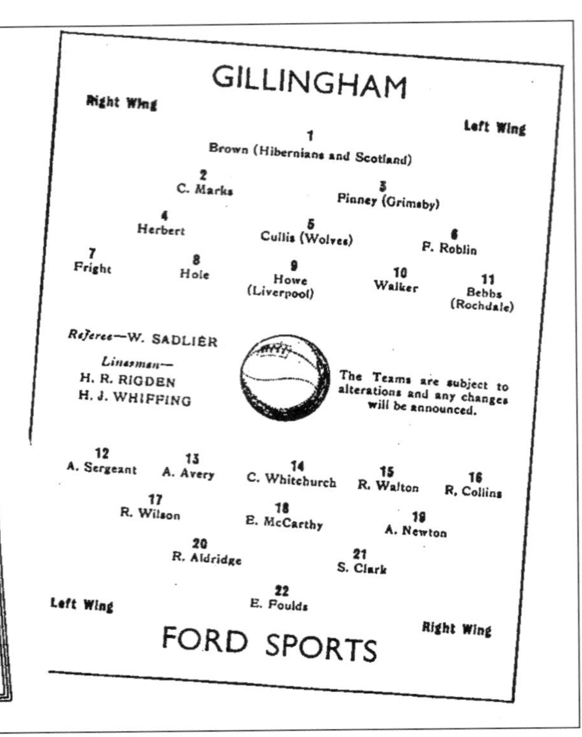

GILLINGHAM

Right Wing — Left Wing

1 Brown (Hibernians and Scotland)
2 C. Marks
3 Pinney (Grimsby)
4 Herbert
5 Cullis (Wolves)
6 F. Roblin
7 Fright
8 Hole
9 Howe (Liverpool)
10 Walker
11 Bebbs (Rochdale)

Referee—W. SADLIER
Linesmen—
H. R. RIGDEN
H. J. WHIFFING

The Teams are subject to alterations and any changes will be announced.

12 A. Sergeant
13 A. Avery
14 C. Whitchurch
15 R. Walton
16 R. Collins
17 R. Wilson
18 E. McCarthy
19 A. Newton
20 R. Aldridge
21 S. Clark
22 E. Foulds

Left Wing — Right Wing

FORD SPORTS

The programme that heralded the return of football to Priestfield. Wolves and England centre half Stan Cullis captained Gillingham in a 3-1 defeat against Ford Sports, watched by a crowd of 4,071.

Centre forward Vic Hole finished as top scorer for the club in the Kent League in 1944/45 and 1945/46.

Gillingham's all-conquering side of 1945/46. Champions of the Kent League, they also won the Kent Senior Cup, Kent Senior Shield and Kent League Cup. From left to right, back row: Clark (Manager), Collins (Trainer), Armstrong, Marks, Brown, Chapman, Lillis, Turvey (Assistant Trainer), Fletcher (Secretary). Front row: Martin, Wilson, Price, Hole, Trumper, Ling.

KENT COUNTY FOOTBALL ASSOCIATION

INVICTA

KENT SENIOR CUP FINAL

Maidstone Athletic Ground

Easter Monday, April 22ND, 1946

KICK-OFF : 3.15 P.M.

GILLINGHAM (RED)

RIGHT — LEFT

1 COLLINS GOAL

2 MARKS — 3 CHAPMAN

4 BOSWELL — 5 PRICE — 6 HALES

7 CHAPMAN — 8 WILSON — 9 HOLE — 10 THOMAS — 11 WARSOP

Referee : Mr. J. WELLER (SEVENOAKS)

Linesmen: A. O. GRANT (MAIDSTONE), C. GOODRHEM (DARTFORD)

12 BONNESEN — 13 SLATER — 14 DUNCAN — 15 RICE — 16 SPENCE

17 THORNTON — 18 RANCE — 19 BRENCHLEY

20 FARMER — 21 FOSS

22 KNUDSEN GOAL

LEFT — RIGHT

12th I. T. C. (Canterbury) (YELLOW)

In the event of a draw the replay will take place on Wednesday, May 1st, at the Maidstone Athletic Ground. Kick-Off 6.15 p.m.

Presentation of Cup and Medals will take place at the conclusion of the match by the President of the K.C.F.A., Frank E. Fehr, Esq., O.B.E.

Price 2d.

"KENT MESSENGER," MAIDSTONE.

Two goals each from Dave Thomas and Eddie Chapman, plus one from John Warsap saw Gillingham overwhelm 12th I.T.C. 5-1 in the final of the Kent Senior Cup at Maidstone.

GILLINGHAM FOOTBALL CLUB CO., Ltd.

OFFICIAL PROGRAMME

Secretary— B. W. Fletcher. *Manager*— A. Clark.	GILLINGHAM v. SHORTS SPORTS	*Chairman*— J. J. Knight. Esq. *Vice-Chairman*— W. S. C. Cox, Esq.

SATURDAY, MARCH 23rd, 1946. Price—TWOPENCE.

CLUB NOTES.

Heartiest congratulations to our lads upon their brilliant victory against Gravesend United at Maidstone last Saturday in the Kent Senior Cup (Semi-final) by 2 goals to nil, thanks to splendid goals scored by Tug Wilson and Dave Thomas. The other Semi-final tie between Erith & Belvedere v. 12th I.T.C. is to be played on April 6th.

Our victory last Saturday was deserved because we had the misfortune to have Stan Trumper injured after the first 10 minutes and he was a passenger for the remainder of the game. He very pluckily returned to the field of play at outside right but eventually had to retire in great pain. Stan sustained a nasty groin injury and may be out of the game for several weeks; but it can be assured that every effort will be made to get him fit as soon as possible.

Gravesend United fielded a very strong team and our lads were fully extended with only ten sound players.

It was regrettable that the ground arrangements at Maidstone last week were far from satisfactory, but we have the assurance of the K.C.F.A., that there will not be any cause for complaint when we visit Maidstone on Easter Monday.

We extend thanks to all supporters who travelled to give the lads the necessary vocal encouragement—such enthusiasm is always appreciated.

Today we extend another hearty welcome to our visitors Shorts Sports in the Kent Senior Shield Competition and we are assured that another interesting and hard game will be seen. The winners of today's match will appear in the Final Tie due to be played on May 11th.

Supporters will be interested to know that arrangements are well in hand for our attractive home game on Wednesday April 3rd. with Eastern Command (Full Representative XI.) – Kick-off 3.15 p.m. Many well-known professional players will be included in the Eastern Command XI., including the famous International player Tom Lawton, who was recently transferred to Chelsea from Everton at a substantial fee. Other match details will appear in the local press. **It is hoped that all Supporters will ear-mark this date and broadcast the match to all their friends. We must have a 'bumper' gate for this special occasion.**

Our game with Leytonstone next Saturday has been cancelled in favour of the Kent Amateur Cup (Semi-final), Sheppey United v. R.N. Depot. Kick-off 3.30 p.m. This should be a thrilling game with plenty of excitement.

Don't forget to book the following Matches—

Saturday, March 30th—SHEPPEY UTD. v. R.N. DEPOT. Kent Amateur Cup Semi-final. Kick-off 3.30 p.m.

Wednesday, April 3rd—EASTERN COMMAND. (Full Representative XI.) Kick-off 3.15 p.m.

Saturday, April 6th—BARMING U. v. SWANSCOMBE (Kick-off 3.15). (Kent Minor Cup Semi-final).

1

SHORTS SPORTS F.C.

GROUND—CUXTON ROAD, STROOD

Chairman: A. BATES Esq.

Hon. Secretary: F. W. BALDOCK

OFFICIAL PROGRAMME

PRICE TWOPENCE

SHORTS SPORTS v GILLINGHAM

Saturday, April 6th, 1946

Kick-off 3.15 p.m.

Above left and below: The home programme against local rivals Shorts Sports in the semi-final of the Kent Senior Shield. *Above Right*: The programme cover for the Kent League Cup tie at Shorts.

KENT LEAGUE AND CUP FIXTURES, etc.

1946

Date	Fixture	
Mar. 23	Shorts ... ... (K.S.S. S.F.)	H
30	Gravesend U. (K.L.)	A
30	Sheppey v. R.N. Depot (K.A.C. S.F.)	H
Apr. 3	Eastern Cmd. XI.	H
6	Shorts (K.L. Cup)	A
6	Barming v. Swanscombe (K.M.C. S.F.)	H
13	R. M. Chatham (K.L. Cup)	H
19	Spurs XI.	H
20	R.M. Chatham (K.L. Cup)	A
22	K.S.C. (Final) ... (At Maidstone)	

KENT LEAGUE TABLE.

	P.	W.	D.	L.	Ps.
GILLINGHAM ...	18	16	1	1	33
Folkestone ...	20	12	2	6	26
Gravesend U. ...	17	9	3	5	21
R.M. Chatham ...	20	9	3	8	21
12th I.T.C. ...	20	8	3	9	19
Sheppey Utd. ...	19	9	1	9	19
Lloyds	20	9	0	11	18
Ramsgate Ath. ...	18	6	3	9	15
Shorts Sports ...	17	7	1	9	15
Snowdown C. ...	20	5	1	14	11
Dartford Amtrs.	19	4	2	13	10

GILLINGHAM

Right Wing **Left Wing**

1 L. Collins

2 Marks — 3 Chapman

4 Henson — 5 R. Price — 6 W. Hales

7 A. N. Other — 8 Wilson — 9 Chapman — 10 Thomas — 11 Warsap

Referee— A. FLACK

Linesmen— P. W. VALSLER, W. W. GORHAM

The Teams are subject to alterations and any changes will be announced.

12 Harris or Conley — 13 Lee — 14 Batchelor — 15 Craig — 16 Fright

17 Duhig — 18 Armstrong — 19 Ware

20 Shaw — 21 Robinson

22 Beby

Left Wing **Right Wing**

SHORTS SPORTS

Goal Scorers—Kent League

V. Hole	30	Lillis	2
Trumper	16	R. Price	2
Wilson T.	15	C. Clark	2
Thomas	11	Ling	1
Warsap	8	Martin	1
Chapman (E.)	7	Ravenscroft	1
W. Harrison	3	W. Hales	1
Wilson I.	3	Boswell	1
		T. Lee	1
		Total—105	

Goal Scorers—Other Matches

Wilson T.	18	R. Sampson	3
V. Hole	12	Chapman E.	2
Thomas	9	W. Hales	2
Ravenscroft	6	Lillis	2
Butler	5	Herbert	2
K. Allbutt	4	R. Bowen	1
Warsap	5	C. Clark	1
Trumper	4	Henson	1
C. Pascoe	3	Martin	1
Tadman	3	Wilson I.	1
J. Hales	3	G. Lukehurst	1
Ling	3	J. Temblett	1
Marks	1	Total—94	

First-class Amateur players desirous of a trial should apply to the Manager stating full particulars, etc. Applications will be welcomed from any Junior player.

Half-back Jimmy Boswell looks on as 'Tug' Wilson is presented with the Kent Senior Cup, following victory over 12th I.T.C. (Canterbury) at Maidstone.

Inside forward Stan Trumper, who was a regular member of Gillingham's Kent League side between 1944 and 1946.

Official Programme

PRICE — — — TWOPENCE

Gillingham Football Club Co.,Ltd.

Priestfield Road, Gillingham

Saturday, August 24th, 1946

Kent League Clubs' Restoration Fund.

REDS

VERSUS

BLUES

KICK-OFF 3.15 p.m.

NEXT HOME MATCHES—

August 31st, Kick-off 3.15 p.m. Kent League

MARGATE

September 7th, Kick-off 3.15 p.m. Southern League

BARRY TOWN

September 14th, Kick-off 3.15 p.m. Southern League

CHELMSFORD CITY

Printed by A. Gibbs, 427, Canterbury St., Gillingham

Left: The cover of the programme for the final trial match before Gillingham embarked on their first season back in the Southern League. *Right*: Half-back George Piper missed just two League games in Gillingham's Southern League championship side of 1946/47.

TAXI SIR !

Phone GILLINGHAM 5704

CENTRAL HIRE SERVICE.

GILLINGHAM FOOTBALL CLUB

Registered Office— (Co., LTD.

PRIESTFIELD ROAD, GILLINGHAM, KENT. Telephone 5854

DIRECTORS—

CHAIRMAN—ALD. J. J. KNIGHT VICE-CHAIRMAN—W. S. C. COX

T. W. BOWMAN, E. T. HAWKES, J. W. LEECH, S. H. MARTIN. G. C. SWAIN.

H. WOOD, A. E. WELLER,

MEDICAL OFFICER—DR. J. MARTIN MALLEY.

SECRETARY—E W. FLETCHER MANAGER—ARCHIE CLARK

Official Programme

PRICE — TWOPENCE

SATURDAY, NOVEMBER 9th, Kick-off 2.45 p.m.

SOUTHERN FOOTBALL LEAGUE

Gillingham v. GLOUCESTER CITY

YOU ARE LISTENING TO Loudspeakers and Amplifiers :: installed and serviced :: BY

RADIO and TELEVISION

RHODES RADIO, 316-8 Canterbury Street, GILLINGHAM.

Telephone - GILLINGHAM 5353

Printed by A. Gibbs, 427, Canterbury St., Gillingham

Left: Prolific goalscorer Hughie Russell scored a remarkable nine goals in the 12-1 home victory over Gloucester City on Saturday 9 November 1946. He finished the season with 42 goals in all competitions. *Right*: The cover of the programme from that remarkable game.

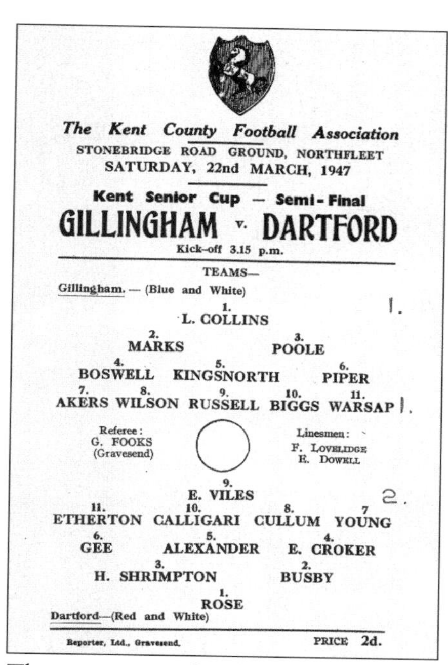

The Kent County Football Association

STONEBRIDGE ROAD GROUND, NORTHFLEET

SATURDAY, 22nd MARCH, 1947

Kent Senior Cup — Semi-Final

GILLINGHAM v. DARTFORD

Kick-off 3.15 p.m.

TEAMS—

Gillingham. — (Blue and White)

1. L. COLLINS

2. MARKS 3. POOLE

4. BOSWELL 5. KINGSNORTH 6. PIPER

7. AKERS 8. WILSON 9. RUSSELL 10. BIGGS 11. WARSAP

Referee: G. FOOKS (Gravesend)

Linesmen: F. LOVELIDGE E. DOWELL

9. E. VILES

11. ETHERTON 10. CALLIGARI 8. CULLUM 7 YOUNG

6. GEE 5. ALEXANDER 4. E. CROKER

3. H. SHRIMPTON 2. BUSBY

1. ROSE

Dartford—(Red and White)

Reporter, Ltd., Gravesend. PRICE 2d.

Left: The programme for the Kent Senior Cup semi-final against Dartford played at Gravesend. Despite a goal by winger John Warsap, Gillingham lost 2-1. *Right*: Warsap was a regular member of Gillingham's Southern League side from 1945 until 1950.

Gillingham's line-up during the 1947/48 season, in which they finished runners-up in the Southern League. The players are, clockwise from top right: Warsap, Akers, Boswell, Poole, Collins, Burke, Marks, Dorling, Kingsnorth, Piper, Forrester, Briggs, Russell, Wilson.

Caricatures of the 1947/48 Gillingham Squad.

Left: Following the death of Jack Knight, Charles Cox was elected chairman in March 1948. He was to hold the position until 1959. *Right*: Stylish inside forward Jackie Briggs joined the club in 1946 after being spotted by Archie Clark playing Army football.

Priestfield Stadium, 1948.

Hughie Russell (9) turns away after netting his second goal in the 2-0 home victory over Worcester City on Saturday 6 December 1947.

Gillingham take the field for their FA Cup tie against Queens Park Rangers on Saturday 10 January 1948. George Piper leads 'Tug' Wilson, John Burke and Jimmy Boswell out for a match that attracted 23,002 to the ground. This is still the club's record attendance.

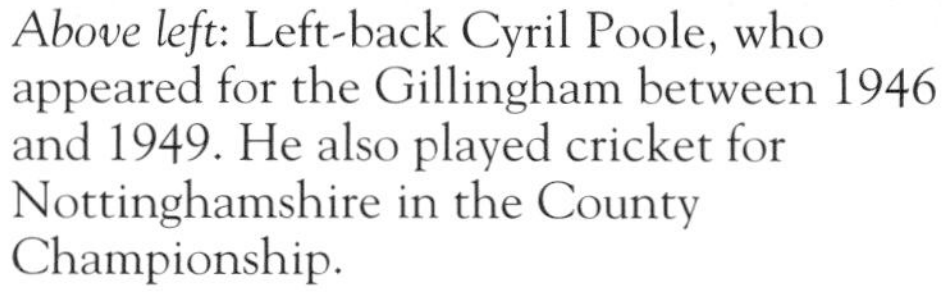

Above left: Left-back Cyril Poole, who appeared for the Gillingham between 1946 and 1949. He also played cricket for Nottinghamshire in the County Championship.

Above right: Experienced goalkeeper Johnny Burke was a regular member of the club's Southern League campaigns between 1947 and 1950.

Right: Former Tottenham full-back George Dorling made over 100 Southern League appearances between 1947 and 1950.

Gillingham players, officials and supporters pictured outside Gillingham Railway Station before embarking on the long trip to Rochdale for an FA Cup tie on Saturday 13 December 1947. The match finished 1-1, with The Gills winning the replay 3-0 seven days later.

Brian Diggins was the reserve centre forward during 1947/48. The form of Hughie Russell restricted him to just two appearances.

Three fringe players in Gillingham's Southern League Championship side of 1948/49 were half-back Trevor Granville (top left), centre half Jack Lambourne (top right) and full-back Len Henson (right).

Gillingham's reserve team of 1949/50. This side finished third in the Eastern Counties League and also reached the final of the league's cup competition, where they lost 4-2 to Chelsea 'A'. From left to right, back row: Millbank, R. Hales, Day, Henson, Armstrong, Trumper, Edmed (Trainer). Front row: Warsap, Bates, W. Hales, Briggs, Poulton.

Victor Cook was the regular reserve goalkeeper during the 1949/50 campaign. Victor did make two Southern League appearances during the season.

In October 1949, Gillingham staggered the football world by spending a fee of nearly £10,000 on three players from Luton Town. They were brothers Charlie Burtenshaw (top left), Bill Burtenshaw (top right) and Bill Collins (right).

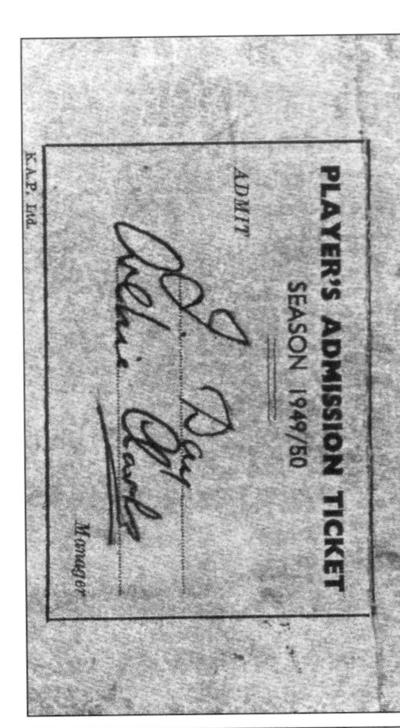

PLAYER'S ADMISSION TICKET

SEASON 1949/50

ADMIT J. Day

Archie Clark

Manager

K.A.P. Ltd.

Gillingham Football Club Co., Ltd.

PRIESTFIELD STADIUM, GILLINGHAM, KENT

Phone : 5854

Chairman — W. S. C. COX

Secretary—E. W. FLETCHER

Manager—A. CLARK

TRAINING RULES AND REGULATIONS

PLAYERS RULES AND INSTRUCTIONS

1. All players to attend on the ground for training each day (except Match days) from 9.45 a.m. and shall be under the orders of the Manager for the rest of the day. Players who are employed at business should attend for training on Tuesday and Thursday evenings from 6-8 p.m. Leave of absence must be obtained from the Manager and such leave will only be granted if the reasons are satisfactory and reasonable.

2. Players will be provided with the necessary outfits for playing and training, so far as practicable. Such outfits are the property of the Club and must be properly cared for. Match jerseys **must not** be used for training purposes. All players are expected to see that their clothing and boots are in good order, if same are not found to be satisfactory the player concerned must immediately report the matter to the Trainer.

3. On Match days all players must be on the ground at least ¾ hour before the time of kick-off, and all players not selected to play **must** attend on match days as above, in case they are urgently required to fill a position caused through an unforeseen emergency.

4. For all Away Matches, the players selected (together with any reserve players) must meet at the place and time stated on the team sheets (subject to any arrangement which may be agreed upon between Manager and player personally) and for that day all players will come under the jurisdiction of the Director in charge of the party or Manager or Trainer or all of them as circumstances may arise.

5. Any case of injury or illness **must** be reported immediately to the Manager and the player shall be under special instructions until declared fit. **These instructions must be strictly adhered to by all Professional and Amateur players.**

6. The Dressing Rooms will be in charge of the Trainer who has **strict** instructions to exclude all unauthorised persons at all times.

7. Gambling of any description is strictly prohibited on the Club's premises.

8. **Players must produce this PASS to the Gateman at the Officials' entrance at all Home matches, otherwise admission may be refused.**

9. All players to be in their place of abode by 10 p.m. on the evenings prior to matches.

10. Players who are away from Gillingham on work will be notified by the Manager on Mondays of each week as to his requirements for the coming Saturday. **All players must inform the Manager by not later than Thursday evening if they are O.K. to play. Phone Gillingham 5854 or postcard.**

11. Players who are in H.M. Service—Rule 10 is also applicable.

REGULATIONS

All notices relating to the selections of the teams and other matters will be posted in the Dressing Room and players must accept this as the only intimation.

NOTE: KEEP YOUR EYES ON THE NOTICE BOARD IN THE DRESSING ROOM.

The Manager is instructed by the Board of Directors to report to them of any infringement of the above Rules. The Directors will deal with such matters as may be deemed necessary and if proved against the player, shall fine the offending player, or suspend payment of wages for a period at their discretion or caution him according to the gravity of the case.

Each player will be provided with a copy of these Rules and he must make himself thoroughly conversant with them as they will be strictly adhered to.

On the field of play all players are expected to be of good behaviour and good sportsmen. Remember that many ladies attend our matches, be clean and tidy in your appearance on the field and uphold the high prestige and dignity of your profession. Avoid all unnecessary waste of time such as kicking the ball after the whistle has gone, etc.

Finally the Board of Directors request and definitely instruct **all** players to refrain from foul play under any circumstances and to accept the Rulings of the Referee and Linesmen without comment or argument.

Always take notice of any advice given by your Captain in the true sportsmanship manner, thereby creating that necessary team spirit which invariably means success to all concerned.

By Order of the Board of Directors,

ARCHIE CLARK,

Manager.

A copy of goalkeeper Jack Day's 'Training Rules & Regulations' for the 1949/50 season. Certain Premier League players could do with having these given to them nowadays!

Four

Back in the Big Time

After twelve years in non-League circles, Gillingham were re-elected to the Football League on Saturday 5 June 1950. The great news was conveyed by a small fleet of cars and the picture above shows the Mayor of Gillingham (George Pinfold) welcoming directors and officials at the borough's boundary.

The Gillingham party pictured outside the Cafe Royal on the morning of Saturday 5 June 1950. Supporters paraded in Regent Street with sandwich boards as delegates arrived for the Football League's annual meeting. It did the trick as Gillingham polled forty-four votes and, along with Colchester United (twenty-eight votes), gained admission to the Southern Section.

OBSERVER

FRIDAY, JUNE 9th, 1950

GLAD TO SEE YOU BACK "GILLS"—VERY

TOWNS BACK ON SOCCER MAP

But the "Gills" are faced with stern task

By DON ELLIS

NOW that the champagne corks have stopped popping and the excitement has begun to die down, it is as well to pause awhile and study the more practical aspects of Gillingham's return to League football.

CHAIRMAN W. S. C. COX

The celebration that followed news of the "Gills" re-admission to the Third Division was amply justified.

It was very definitely an occasion and one that called for rejoicing in a very big way.

Officials and supporters of the club were naturally jubilant. Business people, too, were not slow to realise the importance and possibilities of once more having a League club in the district.

But there is more to it than just that.

When I congratulated Mr. Charles Cox, the "Gills" chairman, immediately after the declaration of the ballot that had ended the Gillingham club's 12 years in the soccer wilderness, I asked him, "What does it feel like to be the chairman of a League club?"

"It feels fine," he replied, "but now our worries begin."

He was right. It is going to be a worrying time for all concerned with the management of the Priestfield Stadium club. The responsibilities of League football are much greater than those associated with the non-League brand of soccer.

FULLY AWARE

That the Gillingham directors were fully aware of their new responsibilities was evident, even at the informal celebration luncheon which they staged in London.

Underlying all the gaiety and the understandable verbal back slapping was a note, not so much of caution as of realisation that a tremendous added responsibility had that day been placed in their hands.

That this would be so had always been realised by Mr. Cox, his fellow directors and manager Archie Clark.

They had invited it and were prepared to accept it. So much so that they were not willing to blink the facts; even at a function that was largely an occasion for rejoicing.

Back home, the more enthusiastic among the "Gills" supporters were talking on the lines of emulating Charlton Athletic and reaching the First Division in three seasons!

In London, Mr. Cox, vice-chairman Joe Leech, and other speakers made no secret of the "Gills" ultimate aim—the provision of even better class football in the Medway Towns.

THEY ARE REALISTS

They did not, however, allow enthusiasm to run away with commonsense. They will put first things first.

And the first and most pressing need will be the provision of a team capable of taking its place in the Third Division when the new season opens on August 19th.

Manager Clark, I am sure, does not expect to set the Third Division alight in the "Gills" first season, or their second either, come to that.

For a couple of seasons, at least, it will be a question of settling down and building a team that will command a reasonably good league position. Somewhere about half-way in the table would be quite a fair start.

Naturally, the "Gills" are expecting very much bigger "gates" for Third Division football. Anything up to 20,000, I should say.

GROUND IMPROVEMENTS

The comfort of these spectators will be one of the chief considerations of the directors.

They will have to consider more covered accommodation, better and bigger stand facilities, more terracing on the slopes.

Other improvements will also become desirable as time goes on.

Naturally, all this cannot be accomplished all at one time.

Of necessity it will have to be treated as something of a long term policy. As will that First Division aim.

First and foremost, the "Gills" will go out to get the team. This will not be exactly an easy task. There is a general shortage of first class players, with transfer fees touching fantastic heights.

Fortunately the "Gills" have at least the nucleus of a reasonably sound side. They will naturally require quite a number of new players to fill certain gaps, and I feel sure that the directors will now insist on a largely full-time playing staff.

This will be essential to meet the sterner test of Third Division football.

Properly organised training, coaching and practice games are an essential to success in modern competitive football.

Already, Manager Clark is engaged on the search for new players. He knows the type of men required and will do his best to see the club gets them.

The "Gills" then, will go forward with high hopes. The task ahead will call for courage and determination.

Disappointments and setbacks there almost certainly will be from time to time, but given the right kind and volume of support there is no reason at all why the club should not firmly re-establish itself in the realm of League football.

It may take a little time, but the possibilities are there and should not be allowed to slip.

The Towns are back on the soccer map.

Let all co-operate to keep them there.

How the *Chatham Observer* welcomed Gillingham back into the Football League.

Manager Archie Clark spent over £10,000 in signing new players for the first season back – and many of these are included in this team picture, which was taken before one of the public trial matches. From left to right, back row: Skivington, Boswell, Henson, Marks, Ayres, Burke, Gage, Kingsnorth, Armstrong, Williams. Third row: Edmed (Trainer), O'Donnell (Trainer), Collins, Russell, W. Burtenshaw, Veck, Lewin, Jenkins, Wright, Briggs, Piper, Day. Second row: McGuire, Fletcher (Secretary), Martin (Director), Weller (Director), Cox (Director), Wood (Director), Clark (Manager), Swan (Assistant Secretary), Dorling, Griffiths (Trainer). Front row: Nobbs, Hales, Carr, Poulton, C. Burtenshaw, Warsap, Trumper, Humphreys.

A crowd of 19,542 packed Priestfield to witness Gillingham's first game against Colchester United, although the occasion was more memorable than the match itself, which finished goal-less.

Gillingham players Ron Lewin, Johnny Warsap, Mike Skivington, Bill Burtenshaw, Charlie Marks, Larry Gage, Charlie Burtenshaw, Harry Ayres, Billy Collins and Randy Jenkins take a break from training.

Goalkeeper Larry Gage was signed from Fulham during the summer of 1950 and he went on to appear in 40 League games that season.

Much work was done at Priestfield to bring it up to Football League standards, the major task being the development of the Gillingham End. The terracing on this side was completely rebuilt.

Bustling centre forward Dave Thomas, who finished as top scorer with 19 goals in Gillingham's first season back in the Football League.

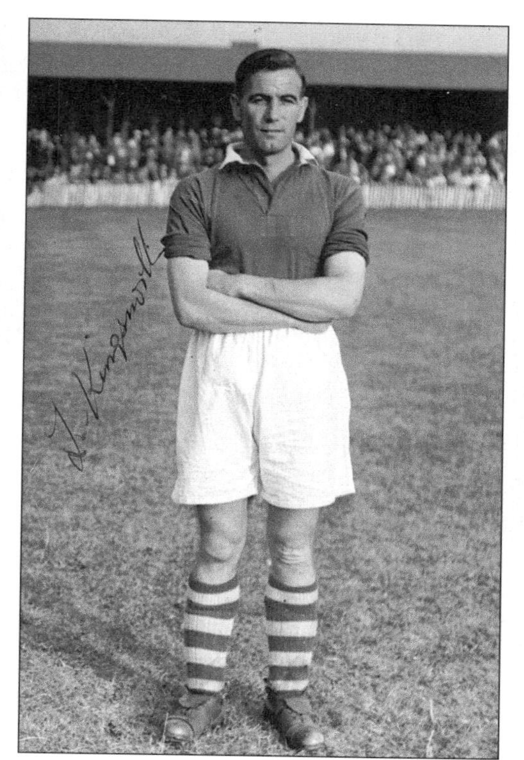

Above left: Dominant centre half Tommy Kingsnorth appeared for Gillingham between 1946 and 1951, having been signed from non-League football.

Above right: Scottish inside forward John Carr made 11 League appearances during the 1950/51 season, having been signed from Alloa Athletic in June 1948.

Right: The front cover of the Supporters Club's 'Priestfield Stadium Review', Volume 2, No. 1 – which heralded Gillingham's return to the Football League. Twelve issues were published from 1948 to 1951 and these are collectors' items today.

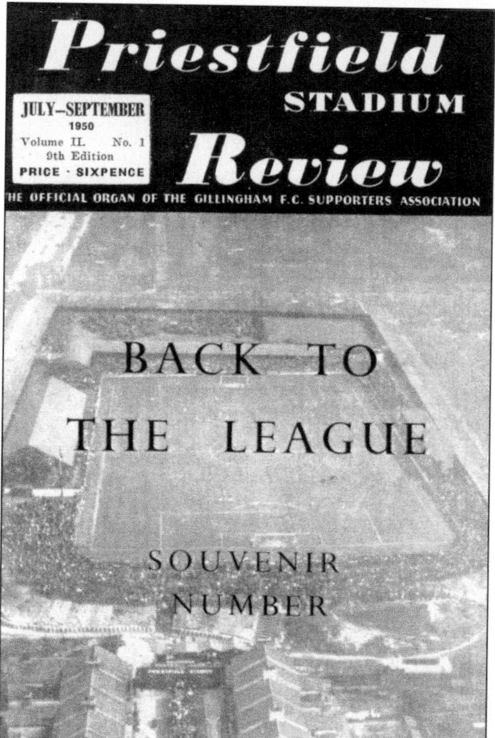
Priestfield
STADIUM
Review
JULY–SEPTEMBER
1950
Volume II. No. 1
9th Edition
PRICE · SIXPENCE
THE OFFICIAL ORGAN OF THE GILLINGHAM F.C. SUPPORTERS ASSOCIATION
BACK TO
THE LEAGUE
SOUVENIR
NUMBER

Centre forward Dave Thomas (9) waits for a slip from the Port Vale goalkeeper in the home game on Saturday 11 November 1950. Thomas scored Gillingham's goal in a 1-1 draw.

Playmaker and inside forward George Forrester served the club from 1947 until 1955.

Above left: Half-back Harry Ayres made 136 League appearances between 1950 and 1955.

Above right: Scottish born Mike Skivington made eight League appearances in the centre half position during the 1950/51 season.

Right: On Wednesday 17 January 1951, Gillingham recorded their record League victory when they defeated Exeter City 9-4 at Priestfield. This is the cover of the programme for that game.

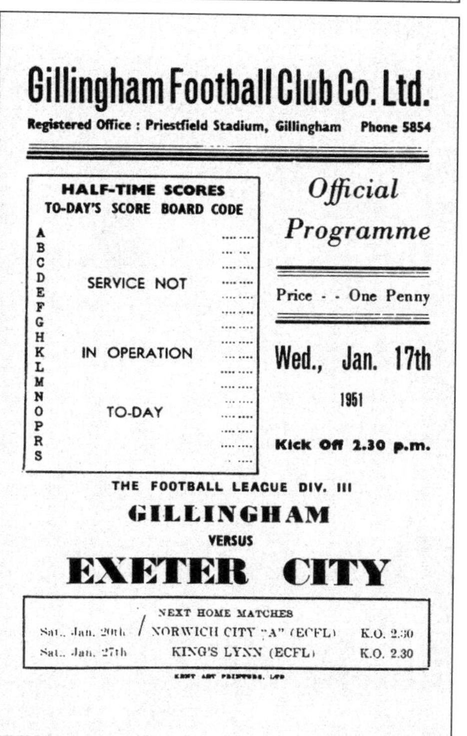

Gillingham Football Club Co. Ltd.

Registered Office : Priestfield Stadium, Gillingham Phone 5854

HALF-TIME SCORES
TO-DAY'S SCORE BOARD CODE

A B C D E F G H K L M N O P R S

SERVICE NOT IN OPERATION TO-DAY

Official Programme

Price - - One Penny

Wed., Jan. 17th 1951

Kick Off 2.30 p.m.

THE FOOTBALL LEAGUE DIV. III

GILLINGHAM

VERSUS

EXETER CITY

NEXT HOME MATCHES

Sat., Jan. 20th	NORWICH CITY "A" (ECFL)	K.O. 2.30
Sat., Jan. 27th	KING'S LYNN (ECFL)	K.O. 2.30

Gillingham FC, 1951/52. This was a far better season than the last, which was mainly thanks to a much better defensive display, although the club needed victory in the last game of the season to avoid re-election. From left to right, back row: Forrester, Lewin, Thomas, Lewis, Boswell, Marks, Rigg, Niblett, Ayres, Russell, Fletcher (Secretary), Clark (Manager). Front row: O'Donnell (Trainer), Briggs, Wood, Leech, Cox, Martin, Weller (Directors), Hillman.

Goalscoring sensation Derek Lewis finished as top scorer for the 'Gills' during the 1951/52 season, with 22 League goals in just 28 appearances. It was not a surprise when he was transferred for a large fee (£12,999) to Division One club Preston North End in February 1952. Whilst at Deepdale, he won an England 'B' cap. Full international honours loomed, until he tragically died from illness in August 1953.

Gillingham Reserves, 1951/52. This team completed the double in the Eastern Counties League. From left to right, back row: Warsap, W. Burtenshaw, Murray, Henson, Bean, R. Hales, Baldwin, Freeman, Edmed (Trainer), Collins (Assistant Trainer). Front row: Weller (Director), Fletcher (Secretary), Kelly, W. Hales, McGuire, Poulton, Wood (Director), Martin (Director).

Full-back John Murray was a regular in the Eastern Counties League side, but also made four League appearances during the 1951/52 season.

Above left: Inside forward Jim Kelly before a reserve team game during 1951/52.

Above right: Centre half Vic Niblett was Gillingham's only ever-present player during the 1951/52 season.

Left: On the other hand, wing-half Joe Baldwin only made a single League appearance in that campaign.

Gillingham before their home game with Brighton & Hove Albion on Saturday 13 December 1952. From left to right, back row: Scarth, Lewin, Boswell, Rigg, Thomas, Marks, O'Donnell (Trainer). Front row: McKee, Sowden, Niblett, Lambert, Long. Jimmy Boswell and Charlie Marks were both ever-present over the course of the 1952/53 season.

Inside forward Jimmy Scarth, who on Saturday 1 November 1952 wrote himself into the record books with the fastest hat-trick in the history of the Football League. Against Leyton Orient at the Rainham End of the ground, he struck in the twentieth, twenty-first and twenty-second minutes. It was later agreed he scored all three goals in exactly two minutes.

Above left: Goalkeeper Tommy Rigg made 192 League appearances between 1951 and 1956.

Above right: Inside forward Ken Lambert finished as joint top-scorer during 1952/53, with 10 goals.

Left: Peter 'Paddy' Sowden became one of the most popular figures at Priestfield during the 1950s. Signed from Hull City in July 1952, he had superb close ball control and could go past opponents with consummate ease. In four seasons with the club, he made 134 League appearances, scoring 27 goals.

Caricatures of the Gillingham side during the 1953/54 season.

The Gillingham FC side that defeated Southampton 2-0 on Saturday 27 February 1954. From left to right, back row: Marks, Boswell, Ayres, Rigg, McKee, Lewin, O'Donnell (Trainer). Front row: Scarth, W. Evans, Morgan, Sowden, Long. The 'Gills' finished in tenth place in the Division Three (South) table in 1953/54 – this was their highest placing since they were re-elected to the Football League.

Experienced inside forward Billy Evans missed just three League appearances during his two seasons with the club (1953/54 and 1954/1955).

The Gillingham FC squad, 1954/55. The team finished the season in fourth place in Division Three (South). From left to right, back row: Kirman, Cherry, Verrall, Niblett, Forrester, A. Evans, Riggs, Kinchin. Third row: Clark (Manager), O'Donnell (Trainer), Roper, Phoenix, Marks, Boswell, Ayres, Rigg, Nekrews, Blake, Edmed (Assistant Trainer), Herd, Griffiths, Probert (Groundstaff). Second row: Morgan, Adey, Lewin, W. Evans, McKee, Warsap, Durkin, Scarth. Front row: Gallagher, West, Lewis, Sowden, Long, Millar.

Left-winger Billy Millar was signed from Swindon Town in July 1953 and, in three seasons with the 'Gills', scored 35 goals in 91 League appearances. In 1955 he won the Professional Footballers' Golf competition on the Moortown course in Leeds.

During the summer of 1955, the playing area at Priestfield was re-levelled. The original slope of the ground can still be seen by the terrace slope at the Gillingham End.

Full-back Bill Parry, who began a long association with the club when he was signed from Tottenham during the summer of 1955. When he departed six years later, he had appeared in Gillingham's League side on 200 occasions.

The Gillingham FC line-up before the home game against Millwall on Saturday 10 September 1955. A 4-3 victory consolidated the club's placing in the top half of the table, a position they held until the end of the season. From left to right, back row: Clark (Manager), Parry, Boswell, Rigg, Riggs, Niblett, West, O'Donnell (Trainer). Front row: Crossan, Phoenix, Sowden, Morgan, Millar, McKee.

Flying Canadian right-winger Errol Crossan, who was Gillingham's only ever-present during the 1955/56 season. He moved to Norwich City during the summer of 1957.

The Gillingham FC team of 1957/58. Six defeats in their first seven games set the pattern for the rest of the season and the club ultimately finished twenty-second in Division Three (South). From left to right, back row: Clark, Fletcher, Parry, Brodie, Boswell, Riggs, Laing. Front row: Payne, Saunders, Hannaway, Morgan.

Left: Harry Barratt was appointed manager in November 1957 and thus ended Archie Clark's eighteen years in charge. Previously with Coventry City, where he was chief scout, he believed in hard work and his orders had to be carried out to the letter! He remained in charge at Priestfield until May 1962. *Right*: Captain and wing-half Jimmy Boswell ended his playing career with Gillingham at the end of the 1957/58 season. Signed in July 1946, he appeared in a total of 342 Football League games, as well as 129 Southern and Kent League matches. His 36 FA Cup games still stand as a club record.

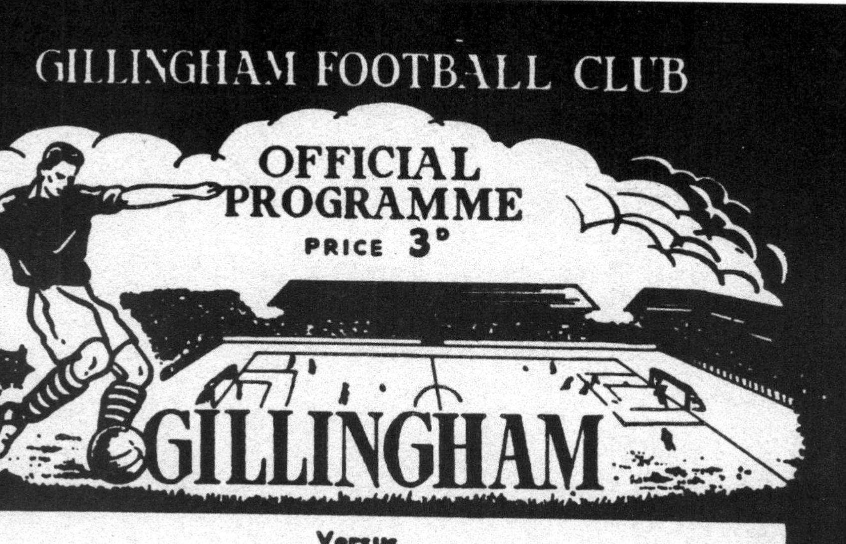

Versus

GORLESTON

Saturday, 16th Nov., 1957 F.A. Cup Competition 1st Round Proper K.O. 2.15 p.m.

TAXIS — 24-hour Service — TAXIS
J. BICKNELL MOTORS Ltd.
77a Gillingham Road : 58 Canterbury Street, Gillingham, Kent
Day Service Day & Night Service
LONG DISTANCE OUR SPECIALITY
Private Hire Coach Automobile Engineers
WEDDINGS COASTAL TRIPS LONDON THEATRES
ANYWHERE :: ANYTIME

J. W. LEECH & SON LTD.
BUILDERS AND DECORATORS
47 KING STREET : ROCHESTER
Telephone : 2662

YOU MAY RELY UPON IT
IT'S PERFECT !
MULTI-BROADCAST
Interference Free Radio Reception

The front cover of the programme against Eastern Counties League side Gorleston in the FA Cup first round on Saturday 16 November 1957. Ron Saunders scored five goals (and missed a penalty) in a 10-1 win. This still remains Gillingham's record victory in the competition.

The squad of 1958/59, pictured before a pre-season public trial match. From left to right, back row: Parry, Smith, Simpson, Moore, Saunders, R. Taylor, Patrick, Hunt, Hannaway, Hughes, Proverbs, Laing, Edgar. Front row: Bacon, Pulley, Payne, D. Taylor, Judges, Laws, Tudor, Read, Sutcliffe.

Left: Centre forward Pat Terry was signed from Swansea Town in October 1958 for a fee of £4,000. During his three years with the club, he had an exceptional record, scoring 60 goals in 108 League appearances. *Right*: Barnsley-born inside forward John Edgar. He finished as top scorer during the 1958/59 season with 23 goals – which included all four in the 4-2 home win against Barrow on Wednesday 10 September.

Gillingham's line-up for the opening match of the 1959/60 season against Gateshead. In a remarkable game, Gillingham won 5-4 with Pat Terry notching a hat-trick. Gillingham eventually finished in seventh place in Division Four. From left to right, back row: Smith, Hughes, Simpson, Proverbs, Albury, Hunt, Parry. Front row: Patrick, Bacon, Payton, Terry, Brown.

Left-back Dennis Hunt was spotted playing in Army football and joined the club in September 1958. Strong in the tackle, he appeared in 321 League games during his ten years with the club.

Gillingham FC, 1960/61. Despite a good start to the campaign, the club faltered during the second half of the season and could only manage one victory in the last eight games. From left to right, back row: Proverbs, Hughes, Simpson, Cockburn, Wilson, Hunt. Front row: Bacon, Shepherd, Terry, Farrall, Brown.

Legendary goalkeeper John Simpson served the club for fifteen years. Signed from Lincoln City in June 1957 for a bargain £750, he went on to appear in a record 571 League games.

The team of 1961/62. Despite four players reaching double figures in goals, it was at the other end where Gillingham had most problems, conceding 94 goals. As a result, the club finished fourth from bottom in the table. From left to right, back row: Ridley, Livesey, Proverbs, J. Simpson, Vaessen, Cockburn, C. Simpson. Front row: Hunt, Hughes, Godfrey, Pulley.

Left: Experienced Scottish centre forward Tom Johnston joined Gillingham from Leyton Orient in September 1961 for a fee of £3,000. He scored on his debut against Millwall and went on to notch 10 goals in 35 League appearances that season. *Right*: Ronnie Waldock arrived the following month, from Middlesbrough. The hard-working inside forward cost £6,000 and he remained at Priestfield until the summer of 1964.

At the end of the 1962/63 season, Gillingham missed out (on goal average) in gaining promotion to Division Three. From left to right, back row: Smith, Vaessen, Livesey, McIntyre, Simpson, Huddart, Hughes, Challis, Farrall, O'Donnell (Trainer). Middle row: Waldock, Wright, Cox (Manager), Hunt, Ridley, Pulley. Front row: Amato, Godfrey, Matthews.

Left: In May 1962, former Arsenal winger Freddie Cox succeeded Harry Barratt as manager. Previously manager of Portsmouth, he was a master tactician and the players he bought to the club knew the pattern and style of play he required. *Right*: Signed from Bournemouth in August 1962, half-back John Arnott stayed six years with Gillingham, during which time he made over 200 first team appearances.

Five

Silverware and Promotion

The 1963/64 squad that won the Division Four Championship. From left to right, back row: Campbell, White, Moss, Ridley, Godfrey, Ballagher, Stacey. Middle row: Taylor, Challis, Hudson, Burgess, Simpson, Hunt, Huddart, Yeo, Smith. Front row: Newman, Arnott, Gibbs, Francis, Stringfellow, Farrall, Pulley.

Gillingham's chairman, Dr Clifford Grossmark, receives the Division Four Championship Trophy from the League's president, Joe Richards, at the Cafe Royal in June 1964.

Left: Ball-playing wing half Alec Farrall captained the 'Gills' to the championship. *Right*: Centre half Mike Burgess was an ever-present during the championship season and helped the club create a new League record of conceding just 30 goals in 46 matches.

Jubilant Gillingham players admire the Division Four trophy at the civic reception. From left to right: Hunt, Stacey, Francis, Gibbs, Burgess, Farrall, Hudson, Newman, Arnott.

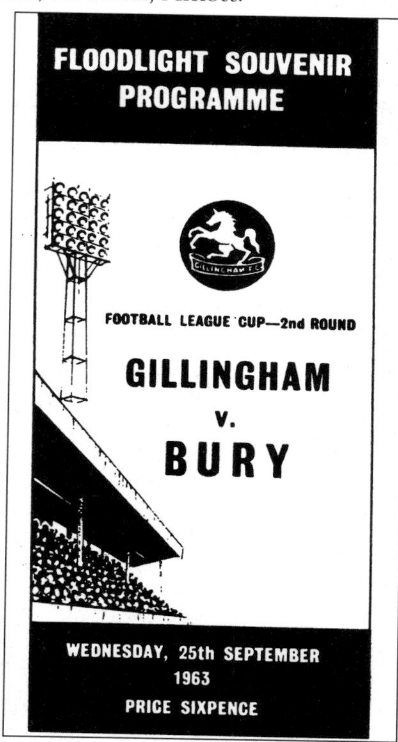

Left: Inside forward Brian Gibbs finished as top scorer at the end of the 1963/64 season, with 17 goals. He also became the first Gillingham player to score 100 League goals. *Right*: The 1963/64 season also saw the introduction of floodlights at Priestfield. They were built at a cost of £14,000. This is the programme cover for the first game under lights. In front of a bumper crowd of 14,979, Gillingham defeated Division Two Bury 3-0.

Key players from the 1963/64 Division Four Championship-winning side were winger Ron Newman (above left), centre forward George Francis (above right) – who scored the goal that clinched the championship at Newport on Thursday 30 April – and experienced right-back Geoff Hudson (bottom left). On their elevation to Division Three, the services of centre forward Rodney Green (bottom right) were secured, for a club record fee of £9,000, from Bradford City. Green went on to score 17 goals, helping the club to seventh position in Division Three.

Gillingham FC, 1965/66. They finished in sixth position in the Division Three table. From left to right, back row: Stocks, Weston, White, Simpson, Miller, Arnott. Front row: Yeo, Taylor, Brown, Gibbs, Rackstraw, Meredith.

Ex-Bedford Town boss Basil Hayward (left) took over from Freddie Cox in January 1966 and one of his first signings was stylish centre forward Bill Brown (right). Brown finished with 10 League goals in 24 appearances during 1965/66.

Gillingham FC, pre-season 1966/67. From left to right, back row: Adig, Gilbert, Woods, O'Mara, Folds, Quirke, Miller. Middle row: Bailey, Weston, Yeo, Rackstraw, Bellotti, Simpson, Ryder, Brown, Gilham, Osborn, Hunt. Front row: Newman, Moffatt, Machin, Arnott, Gibbs, Crickmore, Meredith. On ground: Ridley, Grace, Peach.

Tough tackling full-back Tony Weston. Signed from non-League Bromley, he made his debut during the 1964/65 season and went on to appear in a total of 162 League games.

GILLINGHAM FOOTBALL CLUB

DIVISION IV CHAMPIONS – 1963-64
Members of the Football League, Division III
Football Combination, Division I
Mercia League

SEASON 1966-67

FOOTBALL LEAGUE CUP
2nd ROUND REPLAY

Wednesday 21st Sept. 1966

v.

ARSENAL

Kick-Off 7.30 p.m.

OFFICIAL PROGRAMME 6d.

Inside forward and penalty expert Charlie Rackstraw (top left) arrived during the summer of 1964 from Chesterfield, in exchange for a fee of £4,000. It was one of his penalties that enabled the 'Gills' to hold the mighty Arsenal to a 1-1 draw in the second round (replay) of the Football League Cup during 1966/67. The game attracted a crowd of 20,566 to Priestfield and the front cover of the programme for the match is shown here (top right). Gillingham had gained a credible 1-1 result in the first game at Highbury, thanks to a goal from flying winger Charlie Crickmore (right). Gillingham eventually bowed out 5-0 in the second replay back at Highbury.

The 1968/69 season will be best remembered for the vital point in the final fixture at Shrewsbury Town. A Gordon Riddick goal enabled the 'Gills' to avoid relegation and condemn Northampton Town to Division Four football. From left to right, back row: T. Simpson, Riddick, Williams, Bailey, Gilbert, Simmons, Boswell (Trainer). Middle row: Gibbs, Thear, Green, J. Simpson, Bellotti, Quirke, Hall, Folds, Hayward (Manager). Seated: Woodley, Machin, Yeo, Meredith, Osborn, Weston. Front row: Ribbins, Tydeman, Bray, Peach.

Stylish wing half/full-back Mel Machin (now manager of AFC Bournemouth) was signed from Port Vale during the summer of 1966. After appearing in 156 League matches, he moved to Bournemouth in December 1970 for a £10,000 fee.

Three Gillingham regulars from the late 1960s. Centre half Bill Williams (top left) cost a £7,000 fee to Mansfield Town in September 1967. He went on to make 171 League appearances. Flying winger Derek Woodley (top right) made the short trip from Southend United in January 1968 and appeared in 100 League games for the 'Gills'. Blond centre forward Carl Gilbert (right) scored on his debut against Mansfield in April 1968. Spotted in Army football, he moved to Bristol Rovers in November 1969.

The 1970/71 season turned out to be a disaster! After only one win in their first thirteen matches, Gillingham found themselves in bottom place and remained there for the rest of the season. After an absence of seven years, the club returned to Division Four. From left to right, back row: Hayward (Manager), Ronaldson, Thompson, Bailey, Galvin, J. Simpson, Bellotti, Williams, Green, Tydeman, Folds, T. Simpson (Trainer/Coach). Middle row: Machin, Pound, Smillie, Woodley, Yeo, Peach, Bray, Quirke, Grossmark (Chairman), Knight. Front row: Rogers, Warner, Hill, Keeley, Langford, Housden.

Left: Scottish winger Tommy Watson was signed from Walsall in June 1970. He stayed at Priestfield for two seasons, scoring 7 goals in 49 League appearances. *Right*: Following Basil Hayward's departure in May 1971, Gillingham appointed former Ipswich Town centre half Andy Nelson as manager, in a bid to change fortunes at Priestfield. He certainly did that and within three years the club found themselves back in Division Three.

The Gillingham team that were Division Four runners-up in 1973/74. During the course of the season, the 'Gills' scored 90 League goals – a new club record. From left to right, back row: Galvin, Rogers, Wilks, Richardson, Aitken, Knight, Hill, Tydeman. Middle row: Yeo, Coxhill, Jacks, Jacques, Quirke, Lindsey, Peach. Front: Gibson.

Left: Inside forward and ace goalscorer Brian Yeo. Signed from Portsmouth during the summer of 1963, he scored within five minutes of his League debut. During 1973/74, he equalled the club record of 31 League goals in a season. He eventually finished with 137 League goals in 356 appearances during his time at Priestfield. *Right*: Brian Yeo's strike partner for 1973/74 was Irishman Damien Richardson, who finished the season with 16 League goals. In his nine years with the club, he scored 94 goals in 323 League appearances.

New manager Len Ashurst lines up with the Gillingham squad of 1974/75. Despite a slow start to the season, the club launched a sustained effort from early November to force themselves into the promotion race, although they eventually finished in tenth place in Division Three. From left to right, back row: Ashurst (Manager), Knight, Wiltshire, Shipperley, Hillyard, Galvin, Tydeman, O'Donnell, Toms (Trainer). Middle row: Gregory, Jacks, Richardson, Jacques, Coxhill, Yeo, Wilks. Front row: Lindsey, Fogarty, Swaine, Aitken.

Left: Centre forward Peter Feely, whose signing in October 1974 from Fulham sparked an improvement in Gillingham's fortunes during 1974/75. In 27 League appearances, he scored 16 goals. *Right*: Skilful midfielder Billy Hughes made club history on Tuesday 13 April 1976. Coming on as substitute in the home game against Southend United, he became the youngest player to appear in a Football League match for the club he was only 15 years and 259 days old.

Gillingham FC, 1976/77. Despite a poor period in mid-season (when they lost six games in succession) the team rallied to finish in a final position of twelfth. From left to right, back row: Williams, Hilton, Armstrong, Fogarty. Middle row: Hodgkinson (Assistant Manager), Shipperley, Knight, Hill, Hillyard, Weatherly, Jolley, Galvin, Collins (Trainer). Front row: Muskett, Overton, Tydeman, Summers (Manager), Richardson, Westwood, Durrell.

Left: Former Oxford United manager Gerry Summers was installed at Priestfield in October 1975, after Len Ashurst left for Sheffield Wednesday. In the 1978/79 season he took the club to within one point of promotion, but the 'Gills' never reached such heights again and his contract was not renewed in May 1981. *Right*: Skilful and talented midfielder Dick Tydeman was sold for a club record fee of £65,000 to Charlton Athletic in December 1976. He later returned for a second spell during the summer of 1981 and, in total, made 371 League appearances for the club.

Despite topping the Division Three table in October, Gillingham eventually finished the 1977/78 season in a disappointing seventh place. From left to right, back row: Hughes, Hillyard, Shipperley, Wheatley, Weatherly. Middle row: Collins (Trainer), Crabbe, Walker, Westwood, Jolley, Knight, Clark, Hodgkinson (Assistant Manager). Front row: Williams, Armstrong, Richardson, Summers (Manager), Price, Overton, Nicholl.

Left: Bustling centre forward Ken Price, who was picked up from Southend United for just £2,000 in December 1976. In his seven years at Priestfield, he scored 78 League goals in 255 appearances. *Right*: Another arrival from Southend was midfielder Terry Nicholl. He went on to appear in 184 League games, scoring 11 goals.

Above left: Local lad Graham Knight was a versatile player, who appeared in every position for the club except goalkeeper! He made 245 League appearances for the 'Gills' between 1970 and 1979. *Above right*: John Overton was signed as a midfielder, but found greater success when moved into a central defensive position. So much in fact, that he was voted the club's 'Player of the Year' for the 1977/78 season. *Below left*: Fleet-footed striker Danny Westwood finished as top scorer during 1978/79, with 19 goals. Altogether he scored 74 League goals in 211 appearances. *Below right*: Right-back John Sharpe cost a £30,000 fee to Southampton in October 1978 and was a regular in the side over the next four years. He made 194 League appearances for the club.

Despite the success of the previous season, 1979/80 was a battle against relegation and it was not until the last away game (a 2-0 victory at Chester) that the club made certain of retaining their Division Three status. From left to right, back row: Ford, Armstrong, Hillyard, Short (Scout), Wheatley, Knight, Dudley. Middle row: Hodgkinson (Assistant Manager), White, Overton, Barker, Weatherly, Young, Sharpe, Bruce, Hughes, Collins (Trainer). Front row: Walker, Nicholl, Richardson, Funnell, Summers (Manager), Price, Westwood, Crabbe, Jolley.

Left: Former apprentice Steve Bruce, the central defender, moved on to Manchester United via Norwich City and won every domestic honour in the game. In his time at Gillingham, he made 205 League appearances, scoring 29 goals. *Right*: Inside forward Tony Funnell was signed from Southampton, for a fee of £40,000, in March 1979. In just 12 League appearances, he scored 7 goals that season.

Manager Gerry Summers welcomes striker Trevor Lee to Priestfield. Lee cost a club record fee of £90,000 to Colchester United in December 1980.

Left: Ramsgate-born Mark Weatherly made his debut during the 1974/75 season and marked his first full League game by scoring against Grimsby Town. Equally at home in a defensive or forward position, he made 457 League appearances, scoring 46 times in his fifteen years with the club. *Right*: Keith Peacock was working in America with Tampa Bay Rowdies when he was asked to take over at Gillingham in July 1981. He had spent his entire playing career with Charlton Athletic, for whom he made 567 first team appearances, scoring 107 goals. In August 1965, he had made footballing history when he became the first substitute to be used in a Football League game. In 1986/87, he came close to leading the club into Division Two for the first time ever – but they lost to Swindon Town in the play-offs. Surprisingly sacked in December 1987, he won the Manager of the Month award on five occasions during his stay at Priestfield.

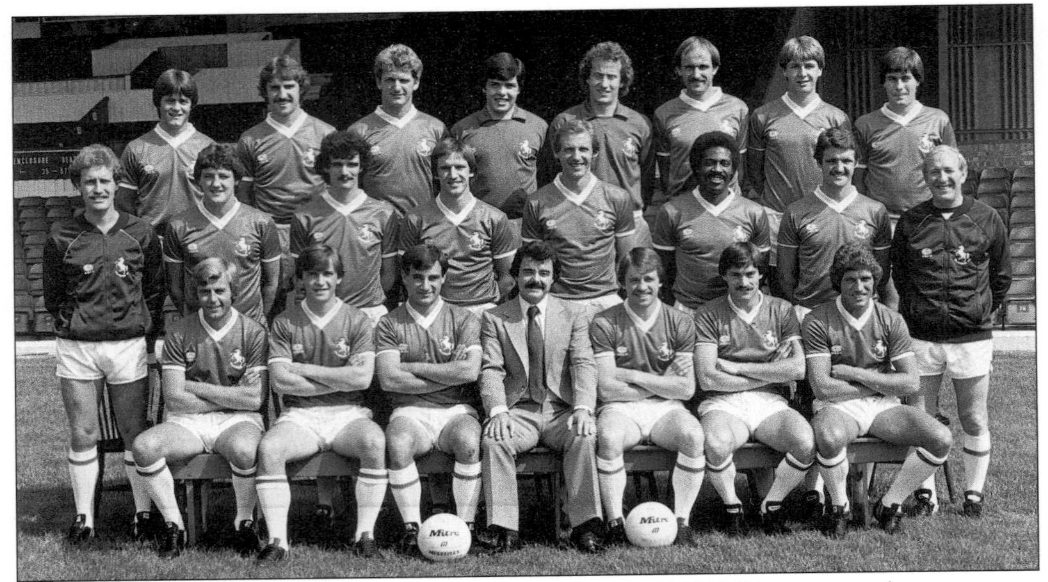

A final position of sixth place in the Division Three table of 1981/82 was a satisfactory start to Keith Peacock's reign as manager. His close season signings included the return of Dick Tydeman from Charlton, along with his team-mate Colin Powell. Midfielder Richie Bowman also arrived from Reading. From left to right, back row: Adams, Sharpe, White, Sutton, Hillyard, Ford, Donn, D. Young. Middle row: Taylor (Assistant Manager), Bruce, C. Young, Henderson, Tydeman, Lee, Weatherly, Collins (Trainer). Front row: Powell, Walker, Bottiglieri, Peacock (Manager), Duncan, Westwood, Price.

In his first full season (1982/83), striker Tony Cascarino finished as top scorer with 19 goals. Signed from Kent League side Crockenhill in exchange for a set of tracksuits, he developed from a raw youngster into a player with considerable ability. In September 1985 he won his first cap for the Republic of Ireland against Switzerland, which was followed by further appearances that season. After scoring 110 goals in 269 appearances he moved to Millwall in June 1987 for a fee of £225,000, which was followed by big money deals that took him to Aston Villa and Celtic.

Although Gillingham finished in a respectable position of eighth, it will probably be the three FA Cup ties against Everton that most fans will remember the 1983/84 season for. Nearly 4,000 supporters made the journey to Goodison Park, where the 'Gills' held out for a 0-0 draw. The replay at Priestfield also ended in stalemate, but only because of Neville Southall in the Merseysiders' goal. The second replay, also at Priestfield, saw Everton coast home 3-0 and eventually they went on to win the trophy at Wembley. From left to right, back row: Scotting, Woodhead, Collins, Bruce, Weatherly, Sharpe, Sage, Young. Middle row: Taylor (Assistant Manager), Buxton (Chief Scout), Shaw, Stokes, Hillyard, Tydeman, Fry, Sitton, Cascarino, Collins (Trainer). Front row: Johnson, Bowman, Handford, Peacock (Manager), Mehmet, Leslie, Duncan.

On Saturday 12 November 1983 Gillingham Football Club suffered a great loss when their chairman, Dr. Clifford Grossmark, died on his way to watch the club play at Walsall. The 'Doc' had been involved with the club for nearly thirty years, having been originally installed as the club doctor in 1954. Three years later he became a director and, in 1961, took over as chairman from Charles Cox Snr. For twenty-two years he championed the cause of the smaller clubs and was chairman of the Third and Fourth Division clubs from 1968. Seven years on, he became a member of the Football League Management Committee.

The Gillingham squad of 1984/85, that finished in fourth place in the Division Three table. From left to right, back row: Hinnigan, Shaw, Cascarino, Fry, Hillyard, Oakes, Sitton. Middle row: Taylor (Assistant Manager), Collins (Trainer), Sage, Shearer, Sharpe, Shinners, Collins, Weatherly, Buxton (Chief Scout). Front row: Leslie, Micallef, Musker, Peacock (Manager), Mehmet, Johnson, Cochrane.

Left: It is no doubt that if Dave Shearer had remained fit for the whole of the 1984/85 campaign, Gillingham would have achieved their goal of promotion. A natural goalscorer, he made it look easy in front of goal. That season alone, he scored 12 League goals in just 23 appearances. His overall total for the 'Gills' was 50 goals in 119 outings. *Right*: Dave Mehmet was a classy midfielder picked up from Charlton Athletic in March 1983. Previously with Millwall, where he won an FA Youth Cup winners medal, he was made captain and finished as top scorer in 1983-84, with 17 goals.

In February 1986, Gillingham stood in second place in the Division Three table and promotion looked a real possibility. However, a run of six games without a victory saw the club slip down the table and eventually finish in fifth place. Once again so close, but so far. From left to right, back row: Elsey, White, Hillyard, Beeney, Macowat, Mehmet, Sage. Middle row: Taylor (Assistant Manager), Hinnigan, Oakes, Cascarino, Shaw, Collins, Weatherly, Gorman (Youth Coach), Collins (Trainer). Front row: Hales, Shearer, Robinson, Peacock (Manager), Musker, Byrne, Cochrane.

One of three ever-presents during the 1985/86 season, goalkeeper Ron Hillyard served the club between 1974 and 1991. Ice cool under pressure, with a safe pair of hands, he made a club record 657 first team appearances. This included 563 League appearances, just eight short of John Simpson's record.

The Gillingham squad that reached the play-offs in the 1986/87 season. After defeating Sunderland over two legs in the semi-final, the club was just eleven minutes from Division Two football when leading Swindon Town 2-1 on aggregate. The Wiltshire club scrambled an equaliser and went on to win the replay at Selhurst Park 2-0. From left to right, back row: Elsey, Pritchard, Cascarino, Eves, Collins. Middle row: Weatherly, Oakes, Beeney, Taylor (Assistant Manager), Hillyard, Hinnigan, Robinson. Front row: Collins (Trainer), Musker, Westley, Haylock, Peacock (Manager), Pearce, Shearer, Quow, Gorman (Youth Coach).

Winger Howard Pritchard cost a fee of £22,500 to Bristol City in July 1986 and was instrumental in helping the club reach the Division Three play-offs. He finished with 14 goals that season and managed a career total of 23 in 113 appearances for Gillingham.

The 1987/88 season was a disappointment after the previous term and the 'Gills' finished in a mid-table position. After being early pacesetters, they slowly slid down the table, which culminated in a 6-0 defeat at Aldershot at Christmas. That result cost Keith Peacock his job and his assistant Paul Taylor replaced him. From left to right, back row: Elsey, Pritchard, Eves, Haines, Shearer, Smith, Weatherly, Gernon. Middle row: Gorman (Youth Coach), Clarke, Kite, West, Taylor (Assistant Manager), Greenall, Hillyard, Berry, Collins (Trainer). Front row: Shipley, Lovell, Haylock, Peacock (Manager), Luff, Pearce, Quow.

Left: The front cover of the programme for the game against Chesterfield on Saturday 5 September 1987. The Derbyshire club arrived at Priestfield having not conceded a League goal in their opening four games, but Gillingham blew that record away by recording their highest League victory. The 10-0 result was also a record for a Division Three game. *Right*: With 25 League goals, Steve Lovell finished the 1987/88 season as the club's top scorer. He went on to net over 100 goals during his spell at Priestfield.

The Gordon Road stand was pulled down in July 1989. Many football historians believed it was the oldest stand in the Football League, having been built in 1899 by dockyard shipwrights – who were said to have been paid in beer and cigarettes!

Manager Damien Richardson with his Gillingham side of 1990/91. From left to right, back row: Crown, Lovell, Haines, Hillyard, Lim, Heritage, O'Shea, Dunne. Middle row: Mughal (Physiotherapist), Jordan, Palmer, Trusson, Clarke, Beadle, Walker, Collins (Consultant), Machin (Youth Manager). Front row: Johnson, Dempsey, Eeles, Haylock, Richardson (Manager), Manuel, Docker, Kimble, O'Connor.

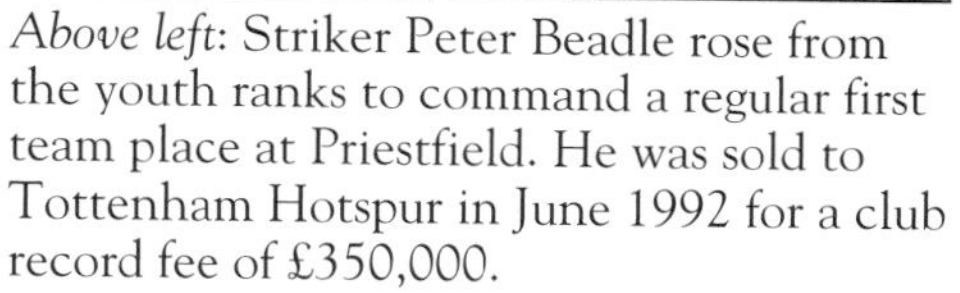

Above left: Striker Peter Beadle rose from the youth ranks to command a regular first team place at Priestfield. He was sold to Tottenham Hotspur in June 1992 for a club record fee of £350,000.

Above right: Welsh midfielder/full-back Karl Elsey had two spells with the club. He will best remembered for his powerful shooting, especially the stinging volley at Swindon in the play-offs of 1986/87. He made 197 first team appearances.

Right: Central defender Richard Green came from Swindon Town in March 1992 and scored twice on his League debut at Cardiff City in a 3-2 victory.

Above left: Glenn Roeder took over as manager from Damien Richardson in October 1992. With the club next to bottom in the Division Three, relegation to the GM Vauxhall Conference looked a real possibility. The former England 'B' international used loan arrangements to the full and eventually helped the club to avoid the dreaded drop. He made 6 League appearances himself that season and, at the age of 37 years and 15 days, became the oldest player to make his Football League debut for the club when he appeared at Scunthorpe United on 28 December 1992. He left at the end of the season to take over the vacant manager's position at his old club Watford. *Above right*: The front cover of the programme for the final home game of the 1992/93 season against Halifax Town, on Saturday 1 May. Probably the club's most important game in their history, Gillingham had a few anxious moments before winning 2-0 and sending the luckless Yorkshire club down. *Left*: It was former youth player and midfielder Tony Eeles who scored the all-important first goal in the victory over Halifax. He struck four minutes into the second half, with a shot from the edge of the area that went in off the underside of the bar. Paul Baker added a second goal thirty minutes later to make the game and, more importantly, the points safe.

Six

A New Beginning

After the doom and gloom of the previous few seasons, it was hoped that, under new owner Paul Scally and manager Tony Pulis, better things would be around the corner. Even the most loyal supporter must have been surprised at the instant change in fortunes during 1995/96. From left to right, back row: Naylor, Dunne, Smith, Carpenter, Stannard, Brown, Lindsey, Micklewhite, O'Connor. Middle row: Jones (Physiotherapist), Arnott, Freeman, Martin, Butler, Harris, Green, Ratcliffe, Bremner (Youth Coach). Front row: Watson, Fortune-West, Wilson, Pulis (Manager), Scally (Chairman), Parsons (Assistant Manager), Bailey, Foster, Rattray.

Above left: New owner and chairman Paul Scally bought the club during the summer of 1995. A businessman from Kent, he has completely turned the club around in his four years in charge.

Above right: Former player Tony Pulis was immediately installed as the new team boss, following Paul Scally's arrival at Priestfield. At the first attempt, he built a side that gained promotion from the Division Three and has proved to be one of the best coaches in the game.

Left: Tony Pulis snapped up midfielder Dave Martin from Bristol City in July 1995 and installed him as club captain. An inspirational figure on the pitch and in the dressing room, Gillingham was the fourth club he had led to promotion.

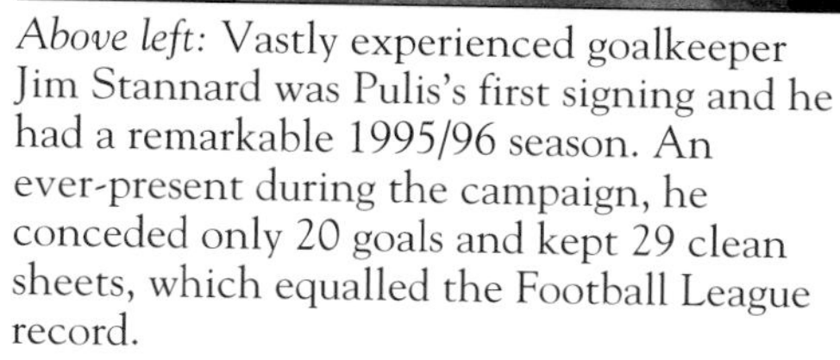
Above left: Vastly experienced goalkeeper Jim Stannard was Pulis's first signing and he had a remarkable 1995/96 season. An ever-present during the campaign, he conceded only 20 goals and kept 29 clean sheets, which equalled the Football League record.

Above right: Dennis Bailey was a £50,000 purchase from Queens Park Rangers in August 1995. His close control and ball-playing ability made him instant hit with the Priestfield supporters during the promotion season.

Right: Tony Butler came up through the ranks at Priestfield. A highly rated central defender, he made 36 League appearances during the promotion season. He joined Blackpool during the summer of 1996 for a fee of £225,000.

Neil Smith, Dave Martin, Leo Fortune-West, Steve Butler, Glen Thomas, Kevin Rattray, Jim Stannard, Paul Watson and Mark Harris celebrate Gillingham's first promotion in twenty years, after defeating Scarborough 1-0 at Priestfield in the final game of the 1995/96 season.

Striker Steve Butler was signed in December 1995 from Cambridge United for a fee of £100,000. The former Army man scored a vital late penalty on his home debut against Plymouth Argyle to put Gillingham top of the table. In January, his second half hat-trick accounted for promotion rivals Chester City 3-1 at Priestfield.

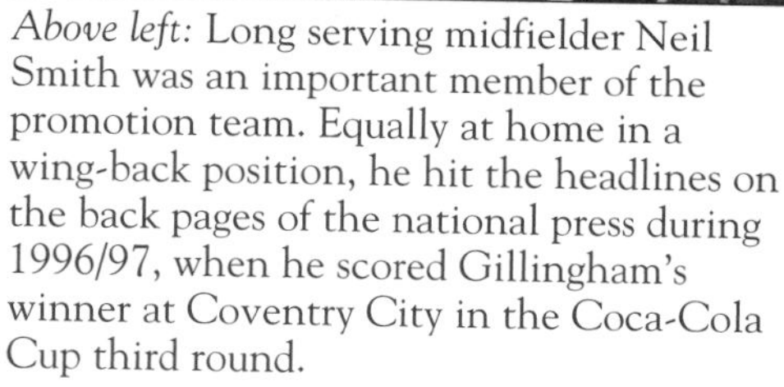

Above left: Long serving midfielder Neil Smith was an important member of the promotion team. Equally at home in a wing-back position, he hit the headlines on the back pages of the national press during 1996/97, when he scored Gillingham's winner at Coventry City in the Coca-Cola Cup third round.

Above right: Mark O'Connor joined Gillingham during the summer of 1995, having previously been with the club from 1989 until 1993. His wing play and close control bought a different dimension to the side, but he had the misfortune to break his leg in a stormy match against Fulham in November 1995.

Right: Midfielder Simon Ratcliffe was signed on a free transfer from Brentford at the same time as Mark O'Connor. Renowned for his powerful long distance shooting, he showed this to great effect in the Coca-Cola Cup ties against Barnsley and Coventry City.

Above: Forward Iffy Onuora was signed from Mansfield Town for a bargain £25,000, just before the start of the 1996/97 season. He was originally used as a winger by Tony Pulis. However, when Leo Fortune-West suffered a broken leg early in the campaign, Iffy was switched to the central position – with great success. On his first appearance in that berth he scored a first-half hat trick against Rotherham and he went on to finish the season as leading marksman with 23 goals.

Left: Andy Hessenthaler cost a club record fee of £225,000 to Watford during the summer of 1996. Although small in stature, he made up for it in commitment and energy in his midfield role. Appointed club captain upon his arrival at Priestfield, he had previously played for his local club Dartford.

The Gillingham squad of 1997/98 that missed out on the play-offs by the number of goals scored. From left to right, back row: Jones (Physiotherapist), Smith, Tydeman, Fortune-West, Edge, Chapman, Bremner (Youth Coach). Middle row: Pulis (Manager), Masters, Ratcliffe, Butters, Green, Stannard, Butler, Thomas, Pennock, Bryant, Parsons (Assistant Manager). Front row: Piper, O'Connor, Bailey, Hessenthaler, Scally (Chairman), Galloway, Akinbiyi, Pinnock, Norman. On the ground: Sinclair, Bovis, Hobbs, Corbett, Radbourne, Osborne.

Tony Pulis had been on the trail of Norwich striker Ade Akinbiyi for nearly six months, when he finally got his man in January 1997. The quicksilver Akinbiyi cost a club record fee of £250,000, but it was to be money well spent. After scoring a superb individual goal on his home debut against Plymouth Argyle, he went onto top the scoring charts for the club in 1997/98 with 22 goals. He moved to Bristol City in June 1998 for a record £1.2 million.

After nearly four months of work, the new Gordon Road stand was opened just in time for the start of the 1997/98 season. These three pictures show the progression that was made from the last game of 1996/97 to it being all ready for the following campaign.

During the summer of 1997, Brentford duo Barry Ashby (above left) and Paul Smith (above right) arrived at Priestfield. Ashby cost £140,000 and Smith £195,000. Smith was rightly named Player of the Year, after being an ever-present during 1997/98. Within the space of a few weeks, Tony Pulis twice broke the transfer record for the club in 1998. First he bought in Bob Taylor (bottom left) from Brentford for £500,000 and then went and purchased his former team-mate at Griffin Park, Carl Asaba (bottom right) from Reading for £600,000.